FOLLOW ME!

FOLLOW ME!

Business Leadership Patton Style

Warren J. Ridge

AMERICAN MANAGEMENT ASSOCIATION

This book is available at a special
discount when ordered in bulk quantities.
For information, contact Special Sales Department,
AMACOM, a division of American Management Association,
135 West 50th Street, New York, NY 10020.

Library of Congress Cataloging-in-Publication Data

Ridge, Warren J.
    Follow me! business leadership patton style.

    Includes index.
    1. Leadership.   2. Management.   3. Patton,
George S. (George Smith), 1885–1945.   I. Title.
HD57.7.R53   1988   658.4'092   88-48025
ISBN 0-8144-5945-5

The author gratefully acknowledges the permission to use material from
the following:

Ayer, Fred, Jr. *Before the Colors Fade*. Boston: Houghton-Mifflin, 1964.

Patton, George S., Jr. *War as I Knew It*. Boston: Houghton-Mifflin, 1947.

Province, Charles M. *The Unknown Patton*. New York: Hippocrene
Books, 1984.

Printing number

10 9 8 7 6 5 4 3 2 1

To my wife,
Joan,
and
my daughter,
Diane,
whose combined persistence, enthusiasm,
and subtle prodding contributed to the completion
of this book.

CONTENTS

PREFACE

As the founder of the George S. Patton, Jr., Historical Society, I have, for the past quarter of a century, researched the life and career of General Patton. I am the author of a book called *The Unknown Patton,* and have written many magazine articles about Patton and the United States Third Army. I have often been asked to lecture on Patton to university students and businesspeople in private industry. I have studied the man and his methods in depth.

After reading Warren Ridge's *Follow Me!,* I made this statement without hesitation: George Patton would have enjoyed the hell out of this book. Not because it focuses on his management practices, but because the fundamental, concrete philosophy offered here is so damned true. Patton's methods and practices as a soldier have much in common with those used by competent and successful businesspeople. The strategies and acumen necessary for daily business operations have more parallels with military experience than most people realize.

Patton's philosophy spans all professions and walks of life. He persevered and continually strove for excellence before such efforts became the subject of management books. He spent his life working, studying, learning, and practicing how to manage people and organizations under the most adverse conditions. He once wrote: ". . . war is organized chaos."

Whether you are a businessperson, artist, baseball player, teacher, soldier, or librarian, you can gain by studying Patton's philosophy.

While reading this book, page after page I found myself nodding my head and thinking, *Ain't that the truth?* As I read further, I conjured mental images of people and business situations I have known, and thought to myself, *That's an exact description of my experience if I ever read one.*

Of course, I know that Warren Ridge wasn't actually writing about my personal experience, but demonstrating the practical applications of Patton's insight and wisdom. I intend to make this book an often-used volume in my business library and believe that it should be required reading for business courses at colleges and universities.

Read this book with an open mind. It will help you analyze yourself, your abilities, and your business performance. You cannot help but learn and benefit.

> Charles M. Province
> Founder, George S. Patton, Jr., Historical Society

ACKNOWLEDGMENTS

I thank retired U.S. Army Lt. Col. George J. Coleman, my close friend, whose first words to me were, "Lieutenant, are you the dumb son-of-a-bitch who's in charge of my deep sea diving detachment, who can't swim?" George introduced me to the views of the good General.

George Peabody Collins III offered me much advice and counsel, as did my son-in-law, Michael King.

To my brother, Jim Ridge, and all the members of the AII whose advice and insight have lent something to this book; I offer my thanks.

A special thanks to Charles M. Province, whose help and freedom to quote liberally from his book, *The Unknown Patton*, was extremely important.

My editor, Eva Weiss, deserves credit for her patient suggestions on organization and arrangement that helped make this book what it is.

INTRODUCTION

General Patton, while attending the Command and General Staff College, Fort Leavenworth, Kansas, in 1924, was presented with a tactical schoolroom problem. His answer was found "unsatisfactory." He carried his unsatisfactory battle plan, maps, and overlays into World War II, and when the same set of circumstances presented themselves in actual combat, he employed his schoolroom solution. The results were excellent. He attached the new battle plan, maps, and overlays to the ones marked "unsatisfactory" and addressed the package to the Commandant, C&GS College, with the message, "I told you it would work you dumb son-of-a-bitch." These words, written in red and signed, "G. S. Patton, Jr.," almost popped through the display case.

Here was a man who had the guts to express the thoughts that I had secretly harbored in numerous business experiences. I had to know more about him.

It seems that just about everybody who had close contact with Patton wrote a book about him. I began reading book after book and began to associate Patton's suggestions, reflections, and actions with daily business happenings. During one confusing management meeting that I attended, the situation under discussion was described as "fluid." I chuckled to myself, remembering Patton's reply to that word when used in a similar context. During the drive on Trier, a staff conclusion was reached that the front was extremely fluid. "You mean," Patton said, "everything is as confused as hell and nobody is really sure where the Germans are. Well, I tell you what I am going to do. I'm going to drive through Trier to see how things are, and then go find out exactly where this damn war is today."

Each instance of management indecision and/or blundering that I witnessed or committed would remind me of a Patton incident. I began to think in terms of what Patton would have done. It seemed to me that he had displayed or recommended ways to effectively treat most business problems and situations. Could Patton's words and actions—when removed from their military context—be successfully applied to business management? Posing this thought to a friend some time ago provoked a forceful response: "You mean to motivate employees you give 'em one upside the head? Or the only good competitor is a dead competitor?" Obviously, he did not believe the business community was ready for Patton's theories.

The thought of George S. Patton as a president of a modern corporation would reduce the student and practitioner of today's management science to apoplexy. The concept of the stern authoritarian with the ivory-handled revolvers simply does not fit the modern approach to management. His theories on war would seem to be totally unsuitable for business. This daring, hell-bent, blood-and-guts character created by movies, reporters, and biographers couldn't possibly mask a brilliant administrator.

Or could it?

He was a great man—few will deny it. But he was a military man. Successful, yet nonpolitical. The niceties of customer relations, the diplomacy of the board room, the pleasantries in many personnel manuals would be alien to this man. He dealt in strategy, tactics, plans, organizations, objectives, people, and surprisingly, the behavioral sciences. What he accomplished were objectives—successfully.

Patton was part Henry Ford, part Bill Lear, part Billy Graham, part Kettering, and part Machiavelli. He could motivate people to do things that accomplished other things. In many ways, he accomplished more than many of our revered management idols. He got there faster with an envied completeness. He was not ruthless. He used the available resources for optimum advantage.

This book will show how Patton's philosophies and techniques are widely applicable to business activities. Indeed, a comparison of such top business executives as Revlon's Charles Revson, RCA's David Sarnoff, Boeing's William M. Allen, Control Data Corporation's Bill Norris, GM's Alfred P. Sloan, Jr., and McDonald's Ray Kroc reveals how Patton capitalized on similar traits and talents, and that he advocated many of the same tactics.

Patton possessed, above all, a keen managerial awareness of what objectives were important and a practical method of how to achieve them. But he also knew how ephemeral that knowledge could be. "It is sad to remember," he said, "that, when anyone has fairly mastered the art of command, the necessity for that art usually expires—either through the termination of the war or through the advanced age of the commander." I hope that by examining Patton's art of command, the more useful of his theories will be remembered and applied by innovative managers as they fit the circumstances.

Chapter 1
GEORGE SMITH PATTON, JR.

When You Are Put in Charge of Something, Run It

You have to turn around and know who she is when fate taps you on the shoulder, because she will. It happens to every man, but damn few times in his life. Then you must decide to follow where she points.

It is not the intent here to create another biography of Patton. But it is important to review, in a thumbnail sketch manner, the years before his fame to measure the impact, if any, they had on his fame. Who was George Patton and what made him tick? How much did his childhood environment contribute to his success? What hardships did he encounter? What or who forged the amazing leadership traits he exhibited?

PATTON'S EARLY DAYS

George Smith Patton, Jr., was reared in San Marino, California, by well-to-do parents, but as a boy he exhibited none of the brilliance that would distinguish his military career. He was a frail child, and his doting parents used his frailty to keep him out of school until he was eleven years old. (Only after that time did he learn to read and write.) In spite of his health—or perhaps because of it—he dreamed of becoming a great general. When he was about eleven years old, he was given a wooden sword, into which he burned the inscription "Lt. Gen. GS Patton, Jr." For an eleven year old to know the different ranks within the general grade is somewhat surprising, but to select the rank at which he accomplished his major achievements defies logic.

Certain ancestors displayed an interest and proficiency in the military, but the family was not steeped in military tradition. His father did read the Greek and Latin classics to George, and the boy developed a fascination for the great battles of antiquity. As his interests broadened, George became engrossed in the study of history and devoured every book he could get his hands on. He had an excellent memory, which allowed him to recall pertinent information at will. As for his physical education, he learned to shoot, ride, and sail, and became proficient at other so-called "gentlemanly sports." Because he was not a natural athlete, he had to work hard and practice long hours. But, even then, George was confident that he could master anything he put his mind to, except perhaps for mathematics, which later caused him to spend an extra year at the Military Academy at West Point.

George graduated from Pasadena High School in California without any special awards or honors. He did, however, display a knack for viewing his deficiencies in a positive light. For example, he was an inferior speller, but in a letter to his nephew, he defended this fault with ingenious logic: "Any idiot can spell a word the same way time after time. But it calls for imagination and is much more distinguished to be able to spell it several different ways, as I do."

Clearly, the characteristics that would make him a good military leader were noticeably present in Patton's youth: determination, confidence, a hint of fatalism, imagination, a desire to learn, and an acute ability to remember (those things that he thought were important) would lead one of the largest military forces ever created to unprecedented success.

MAKING THE MOST OF OPPORTUNITY

As a military man, George Patton was not immediately successful, neither was his climb to power a gradual linear progression. Fate, or luck, had its part, and well-positioned friends lent a hand from time to time. Above all, he was fortunate that the opportunity to command presented itself to him, and he was able to seize the moment. Similar to many business managers, the ability to manage or command cannot be exercised unless the opportunity presents itself.

Patton was a lieutenant at the outbreak of World War I, but he rose quickly in rank. As an aide to General "Black Jack" Pershing, he participated in the Pancho Villa expedition in 1916. His association with Pershing, whom he greatly admired, helped to further his advancement. In France, Pershing made Patton commander of headquarters troops and later assigned him to organize and lead the First Tank Brigade. A serious wound he received in the Meuse-Argonne offensive in 1918 netted Patton the Distinguished Service Cross. He learned well, made new, influential friends, and developed patrons. His exploits were noticed and recorded. He exhibited daring, but not recklessness. Each move was calculated and logical, and his judgment was invariably sound. By the time the Armistice interrupted his meteoric rise, Patton had attained the temporary rank of colonel.

The peacetime army was not to his liking, and Patton was often frustrated by its politics. *Action, movement,* and *excitement* were no longer key words in this vastly diminished defense force, yet he managed his enthusiasm. In so doing, he also developed enemies in his own army. His constant flow of innovative ideas during this "slow period" caused the peacetime apathetic commanders much consternation. An analogy can be made to a company in which apathetic managers mouth the need for innovative spirit while erecting roadblocks to halt any new ideas or proposals. The reason is simple. Innovation requires significant energy and time, and managers may have to assert themselves and put themselves at risk. Most would rather not make waves, conserve energy, and preserve the status quo.

Patton was transferred often—and, indeed, this has been the fate of many a manager whose enthusiasm has alienated his superiors. But when Patton was pushed down in one place, he'd pop up in another. He was often sent to sleepy little posts manned by dispirited soldiers who cared little for discipline, organization, or, for that matter, the military. Within six months Patton would have the best-trained, best-dressed, most effective group of soldiers—and the proudest—in the U.S. Army. He treated war games with a cunningness usually reserved for the real thing, and further infuriated his superiors and contemporaries by winning even when they designed the maneuvers specifically to thwart him. One instance occurred in Louisiana when a two-day maneuver was planned in terrain inhospitable to Patton's tanks. He was expected to quit and surrender because of the total immobility of his armored force. The maneuver was terminated early, but not because Patton acknowledged defeat. His intelligence discovered the location of the headquarters of the opposing general in the game and Patton dispatched one officer and two enlisted men in a jeep up a back road. The three captured the opposing general at pistol point and thus ended the war game. That general never forgave Patton for not following the usual methods in conducting military maneuvers.

Patton treated each situation as a challenge, and by using the basics of management and a touch of creativity, he invariably triumphed over the complex machinations of his adversaries. And what was Patton's secret? He would prevail because he'd adopt an approach that was radically innovative in its simplicity.

Despite his success at winning war games and motivating men, Patton was exiled to a small post "way out west" in hopes that he would become so discouraged he'd retire. It almost worked. Astute military commanders recognized the probability of another war, and minor planning was initiated, but whenever Patton's name was mentioned, his detractors outnumbered and outranked his proponents. His career as a military officer appeared at an end until an influential friend, Gen. George C. Marshall, who was Army Chief of Staff and aware of Patton's combat expertise, intervened.

The interesting aspect of Patton's pre–World War II career is that his accomplishments and failures were typically parallel to those of many business managers. The mild elations, frustrations, and disappointments experienced by middle or new managers relegated most of them to twenty years of status quo or early retirement. The survivors go for the brass ring. In the case of both Patton and the business manager, opportunity is the key.

Without the opportunity to excel, Patton would not have excelled. Without the opportunity to manage, an excellent manager can't prove his ability. Success in management cannot be attributed to stark determination or any other single quality, but rather to some combination of attributes and circumstances. Patton succeeded as a leader by taking advantage of the opportunity when it occurred, and by having an attitude that allowed him to exploit it. He carried out each assignment, regardless of importance, with an unbridled enthusiasm to do the job correctly.

Also, he possessed one invaluable quality that served to motivate his every move—he believed that he was fated to succeed.

HOW TO SUCCEED IN BUSINESS

On November 14, 1980, the results of an in-depth survey conducted by *The Wall Street Journal* were published. It rated the main strengths that determine managerial potential. Over 700 chief executives were interviewed, and the major traits that they considered critical were listed in order of importance. It is not surprising that Patton possessed to an uncommonly high degree many of the traits that were selected.

☐ *Integrity.* This is the trait considered the most important in the survey. Today's headlines most often report malfeasance or crimes caused by its lack. The reputation of business management has suffered from the few obtrusive individuals who take unlawful advantage of their positions, friends, and situations for personal gain. The Yuppie generation and the negative legacy of the "Me" decade have added to the unhealthy portrait of business in the 1980s.

Even Patton's enemies would never suggest that he suffered a lack of integrity. His honesty and incorruptibility were evident in all his actions; in fact, his honesty nearly ended his military career several times when he told his superiors what they needed to know rather than what they wanted to hear. He told it like it was, and he was generally correct. When he was wrong, he had the honesty to admit it. Understandably, he despised gossip, a by-product of integrity's absence:

> *It never does any good and it's unfair. Many men who would never think of hitting a man from behind will nevertheless strike a deadly blow at his character from behind his back. It is the lowest form of sin no matter what cause prompted it.*

In rating Patton on integrity, one would have to give him an A.

There are, sadly, executives who are devoid of ethics and lie repeatedly even though there appears to be no advantage to lying. They use people to massage their own misguided egos and think that all employees can be manipulated with what they've learned in a beginner's course in child psychology. The results of this style of mismanagement are depressing. Often, these people remain in executive positions, and are never exposed for who they are. It certainly gives credence to the old adage, "You can fool some of the people all of the time, and all of the people some of the time, and that's all you need to make a good living."

☐ *Getting along with others.* This is an important, if rather general, trait, and requires specifics for an in-depth evaluation. Unfortunately, "getting along with others" is often used to describe a "do-nothing." It's akin to the expression, "He (she) has got a wonderful personality." You may find yourself suspecting that something is wrong, especially if you think the trait conceals the personality of a "yes-man."

Getting along with others was easy for Patton if you define *others* as other *competent* people who shared with him the same overall objectives. He got along well with his own officers and men, but incompetents, in which classification he included certain members of the higher echelons of command, politicians, media personnel, and Field Marshall Bernard Montgomery. Media personnel were his bane—especially when they reported Patton's cruelty to animals when he found it necessary to shoot donkeys that were blocking a bridge. Patton defended his action as military expedience:

> *The American soldier is absolutely incapable of enforcing the rule that civilians stay off the roads during active operations. His goodness of heart is a credit to him but I am sure it has cost us many casualties. In war, time is vital and bull-carts cause waste of time and therefore death. In Sicily, I was criticized by an ignorant press, who considered it very brutal to kick a few donkeys off bridges, and ignored the fact that by so doing we took Palermo in one day and at very low cost.*

His opinion of politicians was similar to what he thought of members of the news media. He once proposed that anyone who voted for an appropriations bill but failed to vote for the tax measure to pay for it should go to jail. Had his proposal been accepted and implemented, one wonders how many politicians would have ended up behind bars.

Doubtlessly, Patton deserves an A with an asterisk in this category.

☐ *Industriousness.* Patton never learned anything to the point of sufficiency—he mastered it. He was quite confident that he could master anything if he set his mind to it. He was not a natural athlete, yet by perseverance and practice, he mastered sports to the extent that he was chosen as the first American officer to represent the United States in the military pentathlon of the 1912 Olympic Games. He finished fourth in the world. He would have finished first except that in the pistol shooting event, he apparently missed the target completely with one round. Because of his well-known expertise with the pistol, it was later decided that he had fired so accurately that he had placed two rounds through the same hole.

Another instance of his industry was related by his nephew who visited Uncle George when Patton was stationed in Hawaii. Patton had about 500 volumes of mostly history books in his library and the nephew assumed at first that the library was for show purposes only. But in every book he flipped through, he found notations by Patton, such as "the damn fool's a liar—I know because I was there." Without question Patton would score an A+ in this category.

☐ *Intelligence.* Patton's ability to assimilate data and use it in new and productive ways was displayed in every battle he fought. His creative moves even drew respect and admiration from his enemies. In a discussion with a visiting history professor from Harvard, he proved superior in historical accuracy and even bettered Cardinal Spellman on the contents of the Bible. He was incredibly far-sighted and proposed a vision of the future course of world politics that his contemporaries scorned when he predicted the Soviets' intent to dominate the world. But Patton's view proved correct. In intelligence he'd rate an A.

☐ *Business knowledge.* In the business of war, Patton's knowledge was unsurpassed. He was as familiar with the exploits of Hannibal and Caesar as he was with those of Washington, Lee, Grant, and Black Jack Pershing. Military historians marvelled at his total knowledge of military lore. He could discuss weapons, large and small with exact detail, and could speak with authority on any military subject.

A captured German analysis report stated that "General Patton is clearly the number one. He is the most modern, and the only master of offensive. Patton is the most dangerous general on all fronts. The tactics of other generals are well known and countermeasures can be effected against them. Patton's tactics are daring and unpredictable. He fights not only the troops opposing him, but the German Reich."

Gen. Gerd von Rundstedt, the commander of the German forces at Bastogne, said simply, "Patton, he is your best." Even Winston Churchill commented on "the extraordinary military efficiency of General Patton's Army." As for business knowledge, another A for Patton.

☐ *Leadership.* Patton's ability to lead was legendary. It was summed up by his nephew when he said, "There was never the slightest doubt who was in charge when George Patton was around." Retired Army Gen. Robert Williams, a noted intelligence expert, served with Patton until they crossed the Rhine. Williams said that Patton taught him that "when you are put in charge of something, run it. Run it so everyone in the organization knows what they're doing and why." Obviously, Patton excelled at running an organization, and would deserve an A in leadership.

There were two traits omitted from the survey that have, in previous business surveys, been valued highly as indicators of business success. These are sense of humor and decisiveness.

☐ *Sense of humor.* Patton thought a sense of humor was absolutely necessary for mental survival. He used the following vignette often as an example of humor. In 1917, in the town of Bourg, France, the Mayor came to Patton with tears, claiming that Patton failed to tell him of the death of one of Patton's soldiers. After assuring him that none of his men had died, Patton accompanied the Mayor to the "grave." There they found a newly closed latrine pit, with the earth properly banked and a sign saying "Abandoned Rear." Patton didn't have the heart to tell the Mayor the truth, and doffed his cap as a tribute to the fallen commrade. When Patton returned to the same town in 1944, the grave of the national hero, "Abandoned Rear," was still maintained by the natives. Patton's First Armored Corps trained in the western U.S. deserts for eight months prior to landing in North Africa on November 8, 1942, and Patton often would drive around with an aide and make surprise inspections during simulated combat alert conditions. During one such inspection, Patton's aide approached a sentry and asked him the direction from which he could expect trouble. Patton was out of sight but could hear the conversation. The guard pointed to the center of the camp. The aide exploded, "No, No, that's the center of the camp, the enemy would come from the other direction." The guard replied, "The lieutenant didn't mention the enemy—only trouble—and that's where General Patton's headquarters is. That's where I expect trouble." Patton yelled out, "Lieutenant, leave him alone, he knows what he's doing."

In England, some American officers, copying the British, started putting the initials of their decorations after their names. Patton, never known as an anglophile, just added SOB to his signature.

☐ *Decisiveness.* A captured German major general said, "We can always rely on Allied hesitancy to exploit success to give us time to withdraw and regroup in order to slow up the next thrust. But with your General Patton it was different."

With Patton, it was different and he complained bitterly to both Bradley and Ike that Montgomery's indecisiveness had extended the war by several months. Patton's battle cry was "Audacity, Audacity, and then Audacity," and his motto was, "Never take counsel of your fears." His attitude did not permit indecisiveness.

That Patton possessed these excellent managerial traits does not by itself explain his phenomenal success. Some people have all of the listed traits in differing quantities and intensities and most have all but one or two. Perhaps Patton's total commitment to these traits can provide a partial explanation. At the very least, his commitment provides an inspirational example.

PATTON'S EMOTIONAL SIDE

If George Patton had been a stolid, clinical machine and devoid of human emotions, it might, in part, have accounted for why he was so efficient. Emotions can impede logical action. But Patton did have his share of human frailties. He was not a cold, unflappable leader, a fact that was demonstrated many times, to the chagrin of his commanding officers. He pleaded emotionally to Eisenhower to return him to command after being censured for slapping a soldier, and begged Bradley to put him in charge of the Third Army.

Patton, even though he has been portrayed as a fearless soldier, was not fearless. He thought that only a fool is without fear, and he never thought himself a fool. He understood fear but refused "to take counsel of it." Although an excellent horseman and polo player, he admitted that his knees knocked with fear prior to mounting the horse, but once in the saddle the fear disappeared. Before every battle he experienced fear of failure and fear for his soldier's lives, but by recognizing it and facing it, he was able to overcome his fear and function in a seemingly intrepid manner.

Patton would have agreed with the adage, "Patience is a mild form of mental depression often disguised as a virtue." He was not a very patient man. As a young officer in World War I, Patton exhorted his men with very colorful language to vacate their foxholes and advance. To ascertain enemy positions, he sauntered into no-man's land where both enemy and friendly artillery shells burst around him. His impatience allowed him to overcome his fear, and he stood his ground and loudly cursed the enemy, the weather, his own troops, and everything else that impeded his progress. Through the barrage he heard another officer cursing the same set of impediments, and went over to see who it was. George Patton met Douglas MacArthur.

Patton had sympathy and concern for his men, in spite of the cold, dispassionate picture that newsmen have painted, and was moved to tears many times. Shortly after the war, while he was visiting multiple amputees at Walter Reed Hospital, he burst into tears and said, "By God, if I had been a better general, most of you men wouldn't be here." It was not uncommon for Patton to break down and cry during his constant visits to the wounded, and such intense emotions fostered the infamous slapping incident.

His nephew asked him once why he swaggered around, swore, and made such god-awful statements that got quoted in the press. Patton answered:

> *Okay Freddy, you asked, so I'll tell you. In any war a commander, no matter what his rank, has to send to sure death, nearly everyday, by his own orders, a certain number of men. Some are his personal friends. All are his personal responsibility, to them as his troops, and to their families. Any man with a heart would, then, like to sit down and bawl like a baby, but he can't. So he sticks out his jaw, and swaggers and swears. As for the kind of remarks I made, why sometimes, I just, by God, get carried away by my own eloquence.*

Often in business, an executive's secretary may be the best person to describe the executive. Patton's wartime secretary, Helen Tracy, said, "He was much better looking than George C. Scott, referring to the movie *Patton*. He was very tall and had dimples. I had heard of his outbursts of rage but I only once ever heard him raise his voice to anyone. I know he was stern and I was afraid of him myself when I first met him. He cursed like a trooper and I learned lots of new little words. But underneath all of this blow and bluster, he was really an old softy."

Patton also appreciated the importance of a good secretary. In 1943, Helen Tracy joined the Women's Army Corps, and after several formal requests from the General, she overcame many obstacles to be transferred to Europe and reunited with Patton.

HELP ALONG THE WAY

In his quest for greatness, Patton had a secret weapon. Her name was Beatrice Ayer, and she agreed to marry him after he rode his horse up the steps of her veranda, dismounted majestically, and proposed marriage on bended knee.

George Patton was twenty-four years old when he married Bea and they continued a love affair rivaling in its devotion that of Elizabeth and Robert Browning, the nineteenth-century poets. It was not as poetic, perhaps, but his daily letters to her from overseas showed a respect and love that was deep and rare. Beatrice was tiny in physical stature but her size was offset by courage and more than a bit of tact. She was a published novelist, an accomplished pianist, and also wrote music. She wrote several accepted marches and her "March of the Armored Force" is still the official Second Armored Division March. She was a good athlete and excelled in swimming and sailing. She was also a fine horsewoman, although she died at age 67 from a fall from her horse after going over a jump.

Bea was a constant source of support and understanding for Patton and sometimes when his commanding officer became frustrated with him, the commanding officer would appeal to Bea for help. She, in turn, would urge Patton to do the necessary thing. He always granted her requests.

Bea was a powerful woman. One time, in the foyer of an officer's club, she overheard a Reserve colonel belittle her husband while Patton was parking the car. Bea jumped on his back, knocked him down, and was bouncing his head off the highly polished oak floor when Patton entered and lifted her off her victim. Although many women would defend their husbands, few would respond with the courage and spunk of Mrs. Patton.

It is interesting to contemplate for a moment the amount of importance given to the spouse of an executive when he is honored or written about in regard to some milestone or management coup. It is similar to that homage Bea received as George was marching through Europe. Perhaps the secret revealed by James Barrie in his play, *What Every Woman Knows,* viz., behind every great man is a woman, is praise sufficient for the behind-the-scenes principals.

SUMMARY

Patton wanted to die by "the last bullet in the last battle of the last war." Instead he died from injuries sustained in a freak auto accident on the Autobahn, just outside of Mannheim, Germany. It was December 9, 1945. Just before he died on December 21, 1945, he said, "This is a hell of a way for a soldier to die." He was sixty years old.

Prior to World War II, Patton was not a public figure and his exploits until that time were not generally known to people unfamiliar with military history. But his four years in World War II left an imprint on the world. He was respected and feared by both allies and enemies and loved by many of his men. Surprisingly, many Germans attended his funeral cortège as a mark of respect. When the train carried Patton's body from Heidelberg to Luxembourg, French troops gathered a guard of honor along the tracks in more than a dozen cities and towns, and great crowds of Germans stood bareheaded on a dead cold winter morning between 1 A.M. and 6 A.M. to pay their respects. The small town of Ettelbruck in Luxembourg after more than forty years still celebrates Rememberance Day each year on the last Sunday in June to honor Patton. The festivities take place in Patton Park near a 9-foot bronze statue of the General. The town is nicknamed "Patton Town" and pictures of Patton appear in many of the windows. Many of the townspeople travel to Hamm, a village near Luxembourg City to visit Patton's grave. It is marked by a cross exactly as the rest, but it stands apart from the others, just as the man did.

Since his death, over twenty biographical books and thousands of newspaper and magazine articles have been published; twenty-five years after his death, a top box-office film hit was produced. The memories of his military contemporaries have faded, but interest in George Patton remains high. Perhaps the reason for this is that as time passes, more of his projections and admonitions for the future become reality. Originally, these admonitions and projections were not politically tactful and he was typecast as a warmonger when he advocated a strong defense force. He said that there would always be wars. The pacifists and politicians said he was wrong. Since that time we have witnessed fighting in Korea, Vietnam, Cambodia, Cuba, El Salvador, Lebanon, Israel, Iraq, and Iran— and this is by no means a complete list of the world's trouble spots since 1945. When Patton warned of Russia's desire for world domination, he was chastised by Truman, Eisenhower, and the Department of State. Again he was labeled a warmonger. Since then East Germany, Poland, Romania, Hungry, Yugoslavia, Cuba, and Afghanistan are some of the countries that have fallen under Russian influence.

Patton, because of his comprehensive knowledge of history, could predict the most probable course of action in a given situation with amazing accuracy. Gen. Omar Bradley called it a sixth sense. Others labeled it déjà vu. Patton believed that history tends to repeat itself—it always has. Too many of his predictions based on that understanding have come true.

Chapter 2
DEFINING OBJECTIVES

*Follow Me and I'll Show You
Exactly What I'm Going to Do*

*I have studied the Germans all my life. I have read the
memoirs of his generals and political leaders. I have even
read his philosophies and listened to his music. I have studied in detail the accounts of every damned one of his
battles. I know exactly how he will react under any given
set of circumstances. He hasn't the slightest idea what I'm
going to do. Therefore, when the day comes, I'm going to
whip hell out of him.*

When "management by objectives" became a household item in business
several years ago, a colleague reflected aloud, "I didn't know there was
anything else in business to manage except objectives." He was correct.
Objectives are the reasons management functions exist.

Theoretically, the highest level of business organization, usually the
corporation, establishes and defines the reasons or goals for company
business, i.e., the reason the company was started in the first place. Then
the business functions required to obtain these goals are defined, labeled,
and staffed. These second-level functions, in turn, define the steps business organizations will take to accomplish the goals. The defined steps

become the objectives. This practice descends, level by level until all the steps required have been identified.

This deliberate process may not be obvious in all companies, but if the goals are not understood, then the objectives defined may not add up to the goal. Without the presence of goals and objectives, planning—perhaps the most important function of management—cannot occur effectively, and hasty planning, superficial planning, or no planning will result.

The reason for incomplete planning, or a total lack of it, may well be the absence of *organizational objectives* or an inability to identify the objectives where they exist. Yet many companies will require each organization to develop objectives for the year and standards of performance without defining or identifying the company's goals for the year. As a result the organizational and work planning will usually be stated in such abstract terms that gauging accomplishment will be done through rose-colored glasses.

The best way to set objectives is to study and define the area of interest at such a level that any minor deviation in circumstances will easily be accommodated in the plan. Patton, for example, understood his goal to be "Win the war in Europe" and had no problems identifying his objective.

The General always defined his objectives clearly and transmitted them clearly to his staff. When he planned a campaign he always planned two more in advance. But Patton was such a profound student of the past, that his ability was more probably a result of his belief that history tends to repeat itself. He believed that what was true in Caesar's day is true now. He studied his business diligently and understood his goals thoroughly. With his almost total knowledge of the enemy, attained through diligent and time-consuming studies, his ability to set objectives was markedly enhanced.

In February 1945, at a meeting of his staff, Patton said:

> *I have studied the Germans all my life. I have read the memoirs of his generals and political leaders. I have even read his philosophies and listened to his music. I have studied in detail the accounts of every one of his damned battles. I know exactly how he will react under any given set of circumstances. He hasn't the slightest idea what I'm going to do. Therefore, when the day comes, I'm going to whip hell out of him.*

Patton's studies were not just relegated to Europe. In 1936 and 1937, Patton outlined how he believed the Japanese would attack Pearl Harbor, predicting the sneak dawn attack on a packed harbor on a day of rest. He remembered how the Japanese started their war with Russia and how well it worked. Why wouldn't it work again? Of course, his report was given little credence by his superiors and it was filed away.

Once the General set his objectives, he didn't let little things upset his plan nor adverse criticism slow him down. He had a commitment to his objectives. Indeed, commitment provides another comparison to the business world. Commitment seems to be lacking sometimes in business because commitment requires specifics and, specifics invite measurement. Measurement in theory promotes assessment, and assessment affects salary and career advancement.

Foresight in setting management objectives probably could be obtained by an intensive study of past management blunders, management successes, and the competition. Once set, the importance of the objectives cannot be undermined by the fear of failure or any other obstacles to success. Often, it appears that there is a considerably larger management cult that has as its credo, "He who aims at nothing seldom misses."

THE PLAN AND ITS IMPORTANCE

The term "planner" in many business circles seems to have the connotation of nondoer, someone who sits and plans the accomplishments of others. All too often, the connotation is correct. In our age of specialization, planning has in many ways been left to the relatively few, the "planners." There are production planning departments, long-range planning departments, market planning departments, and somewhere, a plans planning department probably exists. It's not that these functions are unnecessary—in most cases they are of benefit. But with this advent of planning organizations, the average manager sometimes thinks that the function of planning is no longer his responsibility.

Many believe the function of planning is a simple but time-consuming annual task, and unfortunately some managers employ this function in a realistic and meaningful manner only once a year. And no, it's not at budget time. The talent in exercising this function is most noticeable in late spring as the manager prepares for his annual vacation. The thoroughness of the planning, which includes investigating every alternative, would amaze the planners of the Normandy invasion. Every transportation schedule is checked and rechecked, and an hour a day is spent on the phone with the travel agent. Vacation plans are explained in detail to associates in the office, the secretary, and anyone else who will listen. It's not that managers don't believe in planning, they do—they believe in vacation planning.

Often, business managers do not believe in business planning. To them planning is not a dynamic, continuing, function: "Planning? Let the ivory tower boys take care of that," the manager thinks. "I'll just get the job done." But if managers don't plan, and don't set planning objectives, how will they know when the job is done? If you are going somewhere but you don't know where, how do you know you're there when you arrive? Planning is the first and the most important function of management, for without planning, there is nothing for which to organize and no one to motivate. Without a plan there can't be a control function since what is controlled is the plan.

Patton was a master planner. He always seemed to attain the optimum—never too little, never too much—and to find the specific balance necessary to accommodate the particular situation. Beyond the ability to establish objectives, devise plans, and ensure derivative planning, Patton had the foresight to calculate the conditions that would exist *after* the objectives were met.

The intent of Patton's reflections, suggestions, and demonstrations of the excellent use of planning is probably contained in one of the many textbooks on management, but probably not with the clarity of meaning and the ease of interpretation that the General attained. Studying Patton's actions results in concrete and practical applications whereby the textbook provides theory.

HOW MUCH IS ENOUGH?

Many business organizations spend a significant amount of time engaged in the function of planning. The budgeting process used in some companies is an example. Budgeting has been termed the most important planning tool in the bag of management science techniques. And well it could be, if its use in any way resembled textbook theory. The student of budgeting soon discovers that an abyss exists between theory and application.

Budgeting evolved from a simple informal attempt to estimate costs into a highly complex, rule-laden affair. With the advent of the computer and university courses in budgeting, a whole new methodology took form.

The budgeting process begins four or five months before the budget period. Instructions are prepared, budget forms designed, schedules prepared, and in some cases training sessions conducted. The process is initiated by a memo from the controller or the treasurer stating that the budgets must be completed by a specified date. All company effort during the budgeting exercise is directed toward the accumulation of details to justify next year's spending. The required amount of detail often precludes the manager from using experience, history, and industry averages to focus on some of the more arduous aspects of the process. The reasoning behind this detail seems to be that by adding these low-level guesses, a higher degree of validity is achieved in the final guess.

If the budget were prepared only once, the effort expended might not be considered wasteful, but as the veteran manager knows, repetitions of the process will occur at least monthly. Finally, at the beginning of the next budget year, the president will dictate the amount of funds to be allocated and to whom, ending the often wasteful escapade. Patton wrote of a parallel effort regarding the "school" approach to forecasting victory:

> *High academic performance demands infinite intimate knowledge of detail and the qualities requisite to such attainments often inhabit bodies lacking in personality. The striving for such knowledge often engenders the fallacious notion that capacity depends on the power to acquire such details, not the ability to apply them. Students plunge in deeper and even deeper, until like mired mastodons they perish in a morass of knowledge where they first browsed for sustenance.*

On the other hand a plan without sufficient detail can also be considered wasteful in that it will undoubtedly be useless.

TIMING

Patton, realizing that the sufficiency of detail in a plan must be benefitted by the timing of circumstances, said:

The best is the enemy of the good. By this I mean that a good plan violently executed now is better than a perfect plan next week.

The perfect plan is, unfortunately, the goal of many business managers and they have a tendency to wait until *all* the facts are available before executing a plan. Timing seems to be secondary. Introducing a new product to the marketplace is a good example of timing. The plan may require that every bug or problem be eliminated prior to the new product announcements because some other company went bankrupt after introducing a product with very low reliability factors. But in today's marketplace, attaining the perfect product may result in the introduction of one that is obsolete. The perfect plan does eliminate risk, which, after all, is what the mediocre manager really seeks to avoid. But when all the facts are available, the need for the plan in most instances will have long passed. Planning is an attempt to make things happen that otherwise would be left to chance, and planning the future is, at best, imperfect. The available facts should be used to develop the plan and then the plan should be executed at the time needed, with enthusiasm.

General Patton thought that Field Marshal Montgomery always waited for the perfect plan and, by doing so, lost many chances to exploit the enemy's position. When both were vying to take Messina during the Sicilian invasion, Patton advanced rapidly while Monty hardly moved at all. Patton, nearing Messina, sent a five-gallon jerry can of gasoline back to Monty with the message, "Although sadly short of gasoline myself, I know of your admiration for our equipment, and can spare you this five gallons. It will be more than enough to take you as far as you will probably advance in the next two days."

Patton also thought that Monty's plans, in addition to being too detailed, were never executed with sufficient zeal. Upon approaching the center of the Siegfried Line, Patton had to give up several divisions to Monty. Patton was piqued, and to release his anger, he jumped up and mimicked Monty giving a staff briefing: "I shall withdraw and regroup, thereby deepening my zone of fire. I shall dispose several divisions on my flank and lie in wait for the Hun. Then, at the proper moment, I shall leap on him like a savage rabbit."

The General, on the other hand, advocated direct action. In September 1944, during his advance to the Rhine, his tanks ran out of fuel. There is a story that his officers, dressed as MPs, diverted fuel trucks from their appointed destinations to Patton's fuel dumps. Supposedly, he himself stood at major intersections and personally directed the drivers to change direction. He wrote of the instance to his wife: "There is current a horrid rumor which officially, of course, I must hope is not true."

Patton's nephew, who was in charge of FBI agent operations in the European theater, visited his uncle at Patton's headquarters in France. Patton complained about being held back for what he considered political reasons and Monty's hold on Eisenhower. Patton told his nephew:

> *Of course, I'm disappointed and damned angry and it's going to cost like hell before we're through. But someday, by God, I'm going to beg, borrow, or steal enough gasoline, ammunition, and air cover to get a big attack going. I've already stolen enough gas to put me in jail for life, but it's no where near enough to keep us rolling. Someday I may even steal a whole damned division of armor and bust the hell out of here. Follow me and I'll show you exactly what I'm going to do.*

Stealing divisions—or, in business, stealing departments or other groups—cannot be advocated as a logical planning alternative and is mentioned here to portray a direct approach and perhaps explain what Patton considered sufficient planning, by which he meant enough to "show you exactly what I'm going to do."

HASTY PLANNING

Haste in business is not uncommon. It is often used as a planning substitute. For those executives, and there are many, who claim that they simply don't have time to plan, haste creates the illusion of progress. "Crises management" it is called, and it is even advocated by some. Books have been written explaining "how to" perform crises management. It's the woodchopper who is so busy chopping wood that he hasn't time to stop and sharpen his axe. More than a few company presidents have secretly admitted the validity of this analogy in their day-to-day operations. They justify it by some instinct they term "seat-of-the-pants" managing. It sounds good. It's forceful, but analysis reveals it as meritless. It's those managers who don't know where they are, and who don't have a good idea of where they're going, who are going to emulate the bold fly-by-the-seat-of-his-pants aviator. They should consider that this practice in aviation gave us the adage, "There are old pilots and bold pilots, but there are no old, bold pilots."

Hasty planning is used only in management. In the medical profession, it is called malpractice; in the legal profession it is negligence; and even in politics, where just about anything goes, it's called malfeasance. In management, haste is often equated to speed. Patton knew the difference:

> Haste and Speed: There is a great difference between these two words. Haste exists when troops are committed without proper reconnaissance. . . . Speed is acquired . . . launching the attack with a predetermined plan.

When an urgent problem presents itself, it is far better to delay hasty, immediate action until a plan is developed. Haste will initiate action faster but will entail redundant and unnecessary effort and will lengthen the time required to solve the problem. Speed (proceeding a plan) may defer initial action but will use the required resources to resolve the problem in a shorter time period.

Hasty management planning is often noticeable when a product defect is detected. It may affect only one unit, but before the problem is defined and alternative actions reviewed, hasty planning will result in closing down the production line, recalling all units from the field, initiating a flurry of failure analysis activity, and fostering charges and countercharges of blame among departments. Since there is an abundance of activity, it is assumed that the problem is being resolved. It may well be resolved in this manner, but the cost and time will be far greater than a planned approach that may begin at a slower rate by defining the problem, locating the problem, and selecting a well thought out planning solution. This kind of approach will expend only those resources needed to devise an efficient process. Admittedly, speed just doesn't seem to have the flair of haste.

PLANNING ASSUMPTIONS

"Worst-case condition" is a term that has worked its way into the jargon of management. Everyone wants to plan for it. Planning for "worst-case condition" seems to be a legacy of the early days of the aerospace industry and manned spaceflights. During the sixties, each part of the total assembly was identified at its origin and each person working on the booster or the capsule was aware that the identified part was to be used to boost or sustain a human being in the mysterious realm of outer space. It was required then, but it spread to unmanned spacecraft and the habit survived the need. "Murphy's Law," a popular adage that says anything that can possibly go wrong will, seems to have spawned a sea of pessimists. Now, all negative contingencies must be viewed as "expected" and what's more, planned for. "Covering all ground" is a common excuse as volumes of planning are developed. Contingency planning is a must, of course, but to itemize, in detail, all of the things that could go awry could demotivate the most enthusiastic manager, which could lead to failure. Planning assumptions should be those that, according to statistics or past experience, are *likely* to happen. The assumptions should reflect "the odds." If the unexpected occurs, recovery planning or replanning are usually less costly to develop, and more likely to promote enthusiastic adherence to the overall objectives.

Patton maintained perspective in the use of planning assumptions especially in directing his staff:

> *When speaking to a junior about the enemy confronting him, always underestimate their strength. You do this because the person in contact with the enemy invariably overestimates their strength to himself, so, if you underestimate it, you probably hit the approximate fact, and also enhance your junior's self-confidence.*

He approximated fact. Just enough—not too much. The parallels in business are plentiful. A new manager's report on the competition will not be tempered by experience and therefore will probably emphasize a relatively negative position for the company. A management auditor, for example, will likely detail only the negative aspects of the audited organization in his or her report because the audit function was devised to discover and point out what is wrong with something rather than to present objective appraisals of both good and bad aspects. When was the last time a General Accounting Office report extolled the positive aspects to offset the negative so as to approach reality. A $250 charge by the contractor for a coffee maker does not necessarily mean that the contractor is cheating the customer. The customer's specifications may be so complex that the charge is indeed a fair price. Each report should be reviewed with perspective, and planning assumptions should reflect the odds.

FITTING THE CIRCUMSTANCES TO THE PLAN

The plan is only a means to achieve the objective. The plan *is not* the objective.

> *The point I am trying to bring out is that one does not plan and then try to make circumstances fit those plans. One tries to make plans fit the circumstances. I think the difference between success and failure in high command depends upon the ability, or lack of it, to do just that.*

Often, a management plan, once devised, is ruled inviolate. It must be followed regardless of the changing circumstances. Managers who revise their plans continually to reflect current conditions are rare, usually because such a practice destroys one of the best alibis for failure. If the plan remains unchanged and were then unsuccessful because of the prevailing business situation, the manager can always claim that the problems were caused by unforseeable circumstances that were not accounted for in the original planning assumptions. The manager's responsibility is limited—he or she may even be absolved—by displaying the ineffectual plan. Who, after all, can forecast fate? And no one will ever think to ask the manager to explain the reasons for not having the plan revised. It just isn't done.

Plans such as these are not merely useless, they're dangerous. If the market shifts, it is much easier to plan to accommodate the shift than it is to push the market back into the plan. But many companies, no longer with us, have done just that. Their attitude has been: "Don't worry about the public, they will come around. Just keep to the plan and produce." Unfortunately, many companies discover too late that this is a hazardous course to pursue. A plan must be a dynamic device that always reflects current conditions.

Work planning has become a popular program in management. Once a year, each employee together with his/her supervisor, establishes a plan for the employee for the year. The plan includes what is to be done and a time schedule for accomplishment. It establishes standards of performance against which the employee can be measured. The progress of the plan is reported periodically. This process logically begins at the highest level of management and descends to the lowest.

The theory, with one major flaw, is excellent. The flaw is that the planning only takes place once a year.

The former president of General Motors, Charles Wilson, observed, "When I see something done the same way for six months, I suspect it. If it is being done the same way for a year, I know damn well it's wrong." If a work plan reflects a year's objectives and is not amended during that time, the plan is either so general in nature that it is meaningless, or it is merely an exercise to satisfy the personnel department. A useful plan must fit the circumstances—and in this day of business dynamics things change rapidly. No longer is product development scheduled in terms of years. It is done in months and sometimes in weeks. With time being measured in micro- and nanoseconds, an organization must react quickly to be profitable.

Sometimes a start-up business plan to be reviewed by potential venture-capital investors will offer a good example of how circumstances can alter a plan. In one instance four plans were prepared, the financial bases of which were in spread sheet form; in each plan the percentage of equity offered to the investors was the same. The venture-capital people would receive X percentage of stock whether they invested $2 million, $2.5 million, $3 million, or $4 million. At the last minute, the $4 million plan was selected because of the investors apparent enthusiasm. Their many accountants reviewed the spread sheets designed for that $4 million plan and judged them reasonable. The sum of $4 million was invested and X percentage of stock was transferred. The circumstances in this case was their enthusiasm, which resulted in a change from the $2 million plan to the $4 million plan.

PLANNING TECHNIQUES

Business managers seem at times to be mesmerized by the techniques of planning while apathetic to the precepts of planning. The solution to all planning problems is often sought in the application of some new and radically different technique. It is only natural to seek innovation—something new, something with flair, something that satisfies the ego and creative needs.

This wonderful aspect of man commonly referred to as human nature is what prompts continual exploration for new and better techniques. Human nature—which is motivated by the innate drives to achieve, to invent, to progress—is responsible for the development of many ingenious planning tools. These tools include spreadsheet analysis, return-on-investment analysis, PERT charting, and systems analysis. They do work and they do save money, which is why they've gained such widespread popularity. Without such innovations the economic, social, and scientific development of the last few decades would have been seriously impaired.

Although human nature inspires us to create and explore, it doesn't inspire us to spend long hours reconsidering the planning that we've done. It is drudgery to review the bland, unexciting functions of planning, and though such diligence may lead to solutions, the task is often equated to "work" rather than "fun." As such, planning review receives minimum attention and effort. To exercise these functions, laborious mental effort is necessary and few of us seek entertainment by these means. As this occurs, the techniques, instead of assisting in the accomplishment of the planning function, become substitutes for the function. When the techniques—through manipulation, blind loyalty, or other reasons—lose their purpose and become the end rather than the means, many costly and wasteful games spring up in business.

As Patton's army approached Vienna, it captured the Imperial Spanish Riding Academy, which had operated in Vienna since the early sixteenth century. The horses were highly trained in a form of equitation that no longer had military importance. In the days of combat by sword, the horses would perform certain gyrations to give the rider more freedom, evasiveness, and force. With the passing of time and changes in the art of war, the purpose of the movements was forgotten and the movements became formalized and acquired a purpose of their own. Patton commented that "people began, as in many other arts, to glorify the means rather than the end which the means were supposed to produce." Management techniques, when followed blindly without regard to the goals they were designed to achieve, can become equally as useless.

PLANNING AIDS

Armies have maps; businesses have charts and graphs. All were designed to help planners visualize conditions or situations so that planning decisions could be made confidently. Sometimes, however, management tends to accept automatically these graphic portrayals as evidence of excellent planning and thorough job knowledge. It's an easy assumption to make. Today just about every activity can be represented by curves and bars, which all too frequently take on a life of their own, and we forget they are just tools and metaphors.

Charts and graphs are designed to summarize and clarify quantities of data, but often they do just the opposite. Presenting a flow chart with several hundred activities and events at a high-level staff meeting will stimulate some employees to study the chart and others to catch up on their sleep. They will not expend the effort to understand it, nor should they. A flow chart showing a maze of interactions that resembles the most complex electronic circuit will induce the same reaction. Each bar, circle, square, or rectangle on the chart or graph may be needed by the chart-maker and understood by him, but when the device is used as an aid to an oral presentation, the mass of detail will frequently defeat the purpose. Often it will merely succeed in obscuring or confusing a situation.

Patton recognized all of those dangers with regard to maps:

> *In my opinion the use of large-scale maps by senior officers*
> *is distinctly detrimental, because by the use of such maps*
> *they get themselves enmeshed in terrain conditions.*

The amount of detail offered should be inversely proportional to the level of management using the data. The more data supplied at higher levels, the more apt the managers are to forget the concepts and become en-meshed in a critical analysis of each piece of data. The use of these aids should reflect the need, and the lower the level of organization, the lower the need becomes. Aids should always facilitate planning; they're not substitutes for it.

Patton believed in augmenting the aid with personal reconnaissance, and that the use of maps below a certain level of organization was of no value, or at least not a replacement for leadership:

> *I have never seen a good battalion commander direct his*
> *units from a map. I have seen many bad battalion com-*
> *manders indulge in this pusillanimous method of command.*

Management executives and employees of many planning organizations cloister themselves in their chart- and graph-infested offices secure with these aids as their basis for planning.

Obviously, Patton did not challenge the efficacy of maps. In fact, he designed and maintained an extraordinary war room. It contained sliding panels along the walls that held small-scale maps of all territories that Patton considered of tactical or strategic interest and included both Allied and enemy positions. Each map was fitted with an acetate cover that was changed continually as new items of information were received so that the very latest in intelligence could be used to aid new planning strategies. It was active on a twenty-four-hour basis. The war room also contained table-mounted contoured models, which had been difficult to build under battle conditions. As his nephew explained, "the General displayed great ingenuity in both theft and improvisation."

SUMMARY

Until the goals and objectives are established, defined, and promulgated, effective planning cannot be devised.

Planning must logically precede all other functions of management for without it, there is nothing to organize for, no reason to motivate employees, and nothing to control. But planning should be designed to accommodate the particular current circumstances in the quality and quantity that conditions permit.

Patton made use of textbook theory, but he established use priorities and methods. He neatly arranged the concepts and explained them in a way that brushed aside the incidentals and forced deliberation on the heart of a problem.

Everything Patton did was part of a plan. Each word, each swaggering step, each tailored uniform were all part of an overall plan to accomplish his objectives. Even his non-country-club language had purpose. He wrote to his nephew:

> *Never be obscene or use profanity in conversation unless the obscenity is so splendid or the profanity so outstanding that people will be so interested that they will forget to be shocked.*

General Patton was truly a master planner:

PATTON SAID:	A GOOD MANAGER:
☐ "The best is the enemy of the good."	☐ Does not wait for the perfect plan.

PATTON SAID:	A GOOD MANAGER:
☐ "There is a difference between haste and speed."	☐ Does not use the "ready, fire, aim" approach.
☐ "Always underestimate the enemy's strength to a junior."	☐ Does not plan for "worst-case" conditions.
☐ "I have studied the Germans all my life."	☐ Studies the past before setting objectives.
☐ "Don't make circumstances fit the plan."	☐ Revises plan or re-plans to reflect current conditions.
☐ "Don't glorify the means."	☐ Uses the planning functions before the planning techniques.
☐ "Be careful using maps."	☐ Does not overuse charts and graphs.

Chapter 3
LEADERSHIP

The Thing That Wins Battles

Leadership is the thing that wins battles. I have it but I'll be damned if I can define it. It probably consists of what you want to do, and then doing it, and getting mad as hell if someone tries to get in your way. Self-confidence and leadership are twin brothers.

Patton probably gave as good a definition of leadership as can be found. He knew he had it because he won battles. Hundreds of other definitions of leadership have been offered over the years, and they all lacked that something—that one definable element that's present in all examples of leadership. The dictionary contains ten different definitions of a leader, but none describes an absolute set of conditions under which leadership can be identified, measured, and quantified.

The concept seems to defy quantification, and one good reason for that may be that the term *leadership* doesn't need to be quantified to be understood. We all recognize it when it is present, but the ingredients seldom seem to follow a prescribed recipe. The results are similar, but the variables in the cause-effect relationship are so numerous that correlation is difficult. Nevertheless, certain attributes and conditions can be identified, and leadership ability can be predicted from the degree of intensity at which these attributes exist. It is probable that the quality of leadership exhibited by a member of middle management are the same as those displayed by an industry leader, but differ in complexion and magnitude.

Patton certainly recognized the importance of leadership:

> *As a mirror shows us not ourselves, but our reflection, so it is with the soul and with leadership. We know these by the acts they inspire or the results they have achieved.*

Much has been published on leadership in an attempt to define and isolate each element of this nebulous trait. Most definitions have failed. Warren Bennis, a professor of business at USC and a co-author of "Leaders," expressed his opinion in a *Los Angeles Times* article of March 6, 1988, which rated the chief executive officer potential of each 1988 presidential candidate. He defined the five qualities that a CEO must have to be successful as (1) technical competence, (2) people skills, (3) conceptual skills, (4) judgment, and (5) character. They were listed in order of least to most important. He defined each quality in subjective terms. For example, he described *judgment* as "that artificial mix of brains and heart that translates into understanding and steadiness." He defined *character* as "ambition, ability and conscience in perfect balance." To each of these five qualities he assigned a quantitative rating on a scale from 1 to 5, which, I suppose, was to make the whole process concrete. Unfortunately, his subclassification of terms such as *understanding, steadiness, ambition, ability,* and *conscience* were themselves abstract in nature, thereby defying absolute quantification.

In a newspaper article on excellence (*San Diego Union*, March 21, 1988), Tom Peters discussed leadership and concluded that it consisted of "good strategic planning, financial wizardry as well as intensity, involvement, and ability to create and bring to life an inspiring vision. . . ." He cited George Patton as saying that "a good plan violently executed now is better than the best plan next week." From this and other examples, Peters concluded that "the essence of management is its emotional side." (I would argue that when Patton made that statement, he was expressing the importance of timeliness and emphasized the word *now.*) Peters suggested that to understand the "emotional" code of management, the reader should change his reading material from nonfiction to fiction, because fiction "examines the nonlinearity of real people who determine the real-world course of our organization." Peters may have had a point, but Patton preferred history with its nonfiction approach to examining the real people who have determined the course of our civilization.

There are hundreds, perhaps thousands, of definitions including one consultant's definition of a good leader as "one who has followers and inspires followers as well." Such a definition may not inspire lengthy scholarly discussion.

Patton made another very interesting observation with regard to leadership:

> *History as written and read does not divulge the source of leadership. Hence its study often induces us to forget its potency.*

The General spent considerable time musing over the concept of leadership, and some of his pronouncements such as "Always do better than what's required of you" or "Fame never yet found a man who waited to be found" could be used to improve the quality of any management seminar.

In leadership discussions and examples, image, motivation, authority, attitude, loyalty, and sometimes tact seem to be a common thread that deserves examination.

ESTABLISHING A REPUTATION

Reputation can be established by a leader prior to an act of leadership, during an act of leadership, or after an act of leadership. A leader's image, based on acts of leadership, is usually formed by others and influenced heavily by each individual's subjective knowledge of those acts. A leader's self-generated image is usually of a positive nature, however, the image created by others may be negative and untrue. The aspiring leader should be aware of the importance of images. They can greatly effect leadership results.

PRESENTING A POSITIVE IMAGE

The following words appeared on a note that Patton sent to his young nephew in 1927, twelve years before Hitler invaded Poland:

This is my war face which I have been practicing before a mirror all my life. I'm going to use it again to scare hell out of the Germans.

Patton could see the war coming, and was creating the image under which he wanted to be viewed. He played different roles to accomplish this, each part carefully and colorfully written for a specific audience. During a 3:00 A.M. discussion over a bottle of bourbon, he mentioned to his nephew, Fred Ayer, Jr., that he was well aware that people asked why he swaggered, swore, wore flashy uniforms, and carried two pistols. He explained that the press and others had built a picture of him and no matter how tired, discouraged, and ill he was he had to live up to the picture. If he didn't he reasoned, his men would say, "The old man's sick, the old son-of-a-bitch has had it," and their confidence and morale would plummet. This role was but one of several, and each role was based on a rational cause-and-effect basis.

The business manager who aspires to a leadership role should create the image of himself that best portrays the dominant traits of that role. One should always be mindful of that exposed position and use the exposure as Patton did—to perfect the image. The image allows followers to know what to expect. When employees know what is expected, anxiety is lessened and leadership becomes more effective.

The manager does not have to face the mirror each morning before work to practice a smile or frown, although some might benefit from it, but one should make a daily, deliberate effort to present a constant image. If the manager wants to be known as the friendly type, he or she should dismiss moods of depression and keep a happy face—by force if need be. If one wants to be a stern taskmaster, smiling, humor, and casualness should be eliminated.

CREATING A NEGATIVE IMAGE— THE SLAPPING INCIDENT

While Patton was leading the largest army ever assembled on an incredible advance across Europe, the media were composing the picture of him that most Americans accepted—the pistol-packing, arrogant, spit-and-polish militarist who slapped shoulders and shot donkeys. Media coverage of Patton was sometimes unflattering and sometimes completely unfactual.

It is not the intent of this book to debunk the media. The purpose is rather to examine the background of one of America's most successful leaders to isolate and identify the traits, events, and circumstances that contributed to his outstanding leadership ability. In passing, though, I hope to dispel some myths and correct some inaccuracies.

The slapping incident is addressed here because of its influence in forming a negative image of leadership, and an erroneous one. The incident was known to all correspondents in the region, but no one reported it because it was considered unimportant or too damaging to Patton's reputation. However, Drew Pearson, sensing a scoop on a slow news day, did report it, and no one seemed to be interested in Patton's explanation or in an eye-witness account. David Currier, a medic on duty in the field hospital at the time gave the following account:

> *The General had been visiting each ward of the hospital and the last ward through which he passed contained some of the most terribly wounded: men missing legs, men with no arms, men blinded or with faces sickeningly smashed. With each he had chatted, handed out cigarettes, took names and addresses so that letters home could be written. The men had done their best to be cheerful. Patton's eyes however, filled with tears and his face quivered. Then he came across a soldier, unwounded, sitting on a packing case, still wearing his helmet. He was weeping and acting in a hysterical manner. This was more than Patton could stand. He did slap him across the face with a glove and tell him to act like a man and go back to his outfit. It was a perfectly normal method of handling a hysterical person, one that many a doctor has used himself.*

As Ayer reflected, "In 1918, George Patton was decorated for his part in an action where he threatened to shoot men who hesitated to advance. In 1943, he was nearly cashiered for slapping a soldier who showed cowardice, or at least hysteria."

Eisenhower was not interested in what had occurred but only what the incident could do to his popularity and political future. Patton had neither the time nor inclination to defend himself and prove his innocence. He took his punishment because he wanted to get back to the job of leading soldiers in battle. His punishment consisted of an apology to the entire Third Army that he exploited to include a motivational tenor.

REPAIRING A NEGATIVE IMAGE

In business, a negative image can be extremely dangerous and it is not something that should be left to take its natural course. A manager's negative image within the company should be changed. The manager should investigate and determine the source of the negative image and if possible repair the image. But the problem should be faced and positive action initiated.

Negative image outside the company—whether influenced by the media or the competition—can be fatal to any leadership role. The appearance of any impropriety should be avoided and corporate leadership roles should be carefully guarded. Internal negative image may damage the leadership, but if conveyed to the stockholders it will be fatal.

The business manager should confront negative image at its first appearance and then create a plan to offset the image as early as possible. A negative image will be more difficult to form if a manager has prepared a strong positive image. In all cases a leader must be aware of the importance of image in leadership.

MOTIVATION

Behavioral sciences in the past forty years have examined human behavior traits from every possible angle. Each investigation and survey seemed to spawn some new and enlightened theory of behavior. Curricula were developed, graduate schools initiated, books published, seminars conducted, and a new consulting field arose. Problems that philosophers, psychologists, and anthropologists had struggled with for centuries had apparently been solved. The "experts" had finally discovered, "What makes Sammy run." Management grasped these new-found truths and at times it seemed that the objective of the company was no longer the quest for profit. Individual fulfillment seemed to replace profit as the prime purpose of company action. If employees refused to perform their assigned work, performed it badly, or just didn't feel like doing it, they were no longer subjected to the practice of reprimand and discharge. They were considered troubled individuals whose happiness and goals were not being realized, and treated with psychological counseling. Thus, employees' happiness became the basis of a manager's performance evaluation. If the manager was not liked, obviously he or she was a poor manager regardless of the work output. (The manager's humanistic virtues were measured on a scale of nine, which gave the rating system an aura of objectivity.) Self realization, interpersonal relationships, and other similar terms became ends rather than means. Understandably, full-scale application of these theories was slightly less than successful. The problems of human behavior survived.

George Patton was not a graduate of any school of human behavior for he preceded this cult by several years. Motivation to Patton was not something that should be laid open to the surgeon's knife in an effort to classify and define all of the elements. Patton was a pragmatist. If it worked, it was good. He was observant and aware, and as a student of history, he observed that certain of a leader's actions obtained certain results from those led. As a human being he was aware that certain stimuli would, in most cases, produce a certain response. Patton realized that if you gave someone a reason for doing something, you had, in effect, motivated him.

The motivation can be positive or negative. A person can be motivated to leave the room by pressing a pistol against his forehead or by promising him a martini and attractive companionship in the next room. In both cases successful motivation is applied, but the latter method would probably be more effective. The best motivation is to get someone to *want* to do what you want that person to do—not simply to do it.

The techniques and philosophy of motivation employed by Patton were far more effective and practical than those normally used in the management arena. The General himself was motivated by challenge, and most of Patton's motivation was in a positive direction. The reasons and examples that he used appealed to pride, justice, fairness, and self-accomplishment—all positive attitudes and virtues. Occasionally he resorted to the negative mode when conditions demanded it. Positive motivation just doesn't work in all cases.

In the drive to break the Siegfried Line and establish a bridgehead over the Rhine, Patton planned an attack despite extremely bad weather and swollen rivers. Hours before the attack, two of his generals argued with him to hold off, but Patton thought that if he discontinued the attack, it would adversely affect the morale of the troops. The generals argued vehemently as the attack hour grew near. Finally, Patton asked them to name their replacements and said that he would keep on relieving until he got someone to lead the attack. They replied that if he felt that way about it, they would continue the attack. The attack was entirely successful. In this situation there was insufficient time to appeal to the positive virtues. Regardless, the generals were motivated and the desired result achieved.

A company's annual report to the stockholders seldom mentions new motivation programs that have been planned or progress in existing programs. It *will* relate, in much detail, planning efforts, organizational efforts, and control devices used. But motivation, the handmaiden of management, is often ignored. Its presence is recognized, but the resources go elsewhere.

Motivating people is neither as complex for the average person to understand as tensor calculus, nor as difficult to perform as a heart transplant. The cost of application is not prohibitive, and yet its lack of use would seem to indicate a high-cost commodity, requiring several years of intensive training to master. It requires an awareness and a deliberate approach.

A daily reminder from a desk calendar, a standard agenda item for staff meetings and communication meetings, or some memory-jogging device, all low-cost techniques, can turn the average leader into an excellent leader. Just minutes a day is all it takes and, if practiced diligently, these techniques become a normal part of each day's operations.

HANDLING AUTHORITY

There have been many masters theses written on the relationship between authority and responsibility and whether authority rests in the order given or the order taken. They do offer interesting reading and pose many problems of an academic nature, but the problems rarely surface in practical application. The real problems seem to relate to misuse of authority—either too much exercised or too little exercised. We have daily reminders in the press in both the business and political arenas. In an impeachment trial of the governor of Arizona in 1988, both conditions were present. The impeaching body found that the governor exercised too much authority when he lent state funds to his auto dealership, and when charged with failing to report campaign contributions correctly, he blamed the whole thing on his brother.

Patton understood the implications of authority. He taught his officers that "when you are put in charge of something, run it. Run it so everyone in the organization knows what they're doing and why."

DELEGATING AUTHORITY

The proper delegation of authority is elusive. Experts tell us that President Reagan delegated too much and that President Carter delegated too little. Yet, there seems to be hardly a primer on management that doesn't treat the subject fully. When is the delegation of authority proper? When it works. The two prime conditions of poor delegation are managing too far down or, not far enough down. Patton clarified the issue:

> *This habit of commanding too far down, I believe, is inculcated at schools and at maneuvers. Actually, a general should command one level down and know the position of units two echelons down.*

Many business schools and management training programs treat "span of control" as a lateral movement only—a simple sideways motion. It doesn't occupy a great amount of emphasis in curriculum. Vertical span of control, if mentioned at all, is allotted even less examination and emphasis and yet its importance in organization is paramount. The effectiveness of the manager can hinge directly on the vertical span of control that is employed. According to Patton, the manager should know the activities of organizations one level down and be aware of the programs and plans of the second level of organization. Some managers succumb to the practice of directing all efforts in their organization. They want to know everything that is going on.

An example of this type of manager is the president of a small electronics firm who each day examines all of the actions of the sales and marketing departments. He questions each employee: "How many orders did we get today? Any returns? Any complaints? How many units did we ship? Why not more?" In the engineering department he wants to know what each engineer is doing and what each draftsperson is doing. This consumes a significant amount of engineering man hours and results in daily overtime and a general feeling that the engineering management is being put down. He strutted through the manufacturing area inspecting an occasional printed circuit board while the assemblers trembled in fear. He does all this not in an effort to develop esprit de corps in the company, but because he feels that he cannot trust anyone else and that no one can do anything as well as he. It also gives him an opportunity to display his power to the assemblers, and display his technical knowledge to engineering personnel. He has a span of control of seven, according to his organization chart, and he has selected each. But, since he spends all of his time duplicating the jobs of his staff in detail, the company lacks a product plan, a long-range plan, and for that matter, any kind of plan. Everyday is crisis management. Patton would not have approved.

In North Africa, Patton reported to Field Marshal Alexander, whom he respected highly. One evening, Alexander called Patton and instructed him to move his Second Division to a certain location. Patton interrupted him to say:

> As my commander, you can order me to march my army into the sea, and I will. But no one, including the Lord Almighty has the right to tell the commander of an army how he shall dispose of his division.

Field Marshal Alexander said, "George, you're absolutely right."

The applicability of this concept to management is another example of managing too far down. The manager should instruct his staff and then they should determine the exact method to best employ their assets and resources.

Conversely, there are some managers that direct only their staff and exhibit a completely laissez-faire attitude below that level. They issue their orders and assume that everything will be done in conformance with their desires. They show no interest in their second-level organizations and do not follow their programs, or plans, or progress. The danger in this mode of management is that if a serious error is committed two levels down, the manager may not become aware of it until it is too late to correct or offset the error.

If a manager directs his staff and in addition knows the objectives, plans, and progress of each unit one level below, he can usually avert the catastrophic blunders. He avoids redundant management and still retains control and perspective of the *most decisive cost level.*

LOYALTY

If forced to choose between loyalty or intelligence in an officer, Patton would not hesitate:

> *I prefer a loyal staff officer to a brilliant one.*

Patton stressed the importance of loyalty as do many companies. In fact, just about all company policy manuals use the words "employee loyalty" often to explain the company's ambiance. When a business situation evolves in which a trusted and valuable employee decides to leave the employ and gives two-week's notice, the manager may describe it as an act of disloyalty because the employee does not consider the adverse impact to the company. Yet, the same manager in a financial cutback would give the same employee his pink slip without any concern for the employee's personal, financial, or emotional position at the time. If asked about the paradoxical situation the manager might say, "the employee's personal business is not our business." But Patton realized that loyalty had to be a two-way street:

> *Loyalty is frequently only considered as faithfulness from the bottom up. It has another and equally important application; that is from the top down. One of the most frequently noted characteristics of the great is unforgetfulness of any loyalty to their subordinates. It is this characteristic which binds, with hoops of iron, their juniors to them.*

These hoops of iron may account for a significant element in leadership success.

So it may well benefit the average manager to view his or her position on loyalty as a bidirectional rather than a unidirectional virtue.

ATTITUDE

Patton knew the importance of a winning attitude, and he knew how to create it:

> *In planning any operation, it is vital to remember, and constantly repeat to oneself two things; In war nothing is impossible, provided you use audacity, and "Do not take counsel of your fears." If these two principles are adhered to . . . victory is certain.*

Beyond these factors that influence the morale of an organization are a leader's intangible qualities that he uses to motivate others. They are usually described under a composite term such as an aura, a certain charisma, a charm, or a captivating personality. They are, in effect, an attitude. An old adage says that habits take us to yesterday's answers and attitude keeps us there. Attitudes can retard advancement but can promote advancement equally as well. The attitude is the sum total of a new person, complete with prejudices, foibles, faith, learning, and a few other things that are, to this point, unidentified. It is a person's outlook on something. It can be glum, apathetic, or hopeful. Whatever it is, it is intuited and often reflected by others. An attitude of anger will create anger in others, happiness will beget happiness, confidence will instill confidence, and enthusiasm will promote enthusiasm. Patton was successful because his attitude demanded success.

In the battle of Trier, a major railhead of a heavily defended German triangle, Patton's superiors did not believe Trier could be taken and would not have given Patton permission for the attack had he asked. He persuaded Gen. Omar Bradley to let him attack until dark, and then got permission to use "an armored reconnaissance in force." There is no such military expression, since "reconnaissance" essentially means looking for enemy positions, and doesn't apply to combat in force. Both Patton and Bradley ignored their telephones to avoid Eisenhower's order to discontinue the attack. By using audacity and a good measure of creativity— German intelligence was totally confused—Patton took Trier in record time. Patton immediately called Bradley and said, "Brad, I just took Trier, what do you want to do, give it back to the Germans?"

Patton recognized fear and experienced it, but his fear never caused indecision. He was well aware that fear of failure is one of the greatest inhibitors to accomplishment. Today there are legions of middle managers who will remain in that category despite their ability to exercise management functions. The engineering manager who reads every engineering journal just to "stay in touch," the manager of finance who adds each set of figures presented "to keep a hand in," and the manager of operations who must verify each detailed shortage report "so something doesn't slip through the crack" are all examples of fear of failure. They are afraid to commit themselves fully to the job of managing and are in a sense practicing their old jobs just in case they don't succeed as managers. They are taking counsel of their fears, and the attitude comes through.

Patton believed that the apparently impossible was overcome by disregarding the normal restraints and using a novel approach. Then, he counseled initiating the approach with an intrepid boldness. Kettering did the same when he developed the self-starter. All electrical engineers knew that the desired current could not be conducted through such thin wire. They had the formulas to prove it. Kettering said it could be done for a brief period—long enough to start the engine. Lear was called mentally troubled when he announced his Lear jet. Everyone knew that there was no market and that it couldn't be built for the stated cost. Lear had the boldness to do it. When the physicists Michaelson and Morely wondered why the ether drift had no apparent effect on their experiment, Einstein, secure in his own confidence, stated simply that there was no such thing as ether drift or wind. All of these accomplishments resulted from the proper attitude.

When simplicity, audacity, confidence, and the ability to overcome his fear were insufficient, George Patton added one more thing. He heeded the advice of another general. Grant once said, "In every battle there comes a time when both sides consider themselves beaten; then he who continues the attack wins." Patton was persistent. He accepted minor setbacks as a normal part of any endeavor and he turned major setbacks into victories with persistence.

> *Often I have encountered in life that great disappointments*
> *have proved to be the road to future successes.*

Patton persisted in learning something from every event. In victory, he wanted to discuss the battles with the defeated generals to learn their opinions. Such a desire to learn demands an open mind.

George Patton's attitude was envied and hated by many of his contemporary American military officers as well as by his enemies. They saw in him something indefinable that they did not possess. They had the qualities and abilities instilled in military schools and by military tradition. He still had the advantage. He had a winning attitude and the ability to motivate his men to accomplish far more than would be normally expected of them.

BOLDNESS

Patton understood the value of boldness:

> *Success in war depends on the golden rules of war: speed,*
> *simplicity, and boldness.*

Boldness is not a word usually used in the management vocabulary. *Aggressive, sure-fisted,* and *strong-willed* are some adjectives used to describe a manager's most valuable quality, but none seems to capture what Patton believed to be boldness, which he saw as a certain mixture of self-confidence and audacity: a willingness to accept risk and take action.

Could it be that success in business depends on speed, simplicity, and boldness?

Hannibal displayed boldness when he crossed the Alps, and Patton used it when he crossed the Alps in a less well-known event. At the end of the war when the situation in Yugoslavia was not clear, the Third Army was ordered to move five divisions into the Fifth Army in the British area south of the Alps, north of Trieste. Immediately, the Third U.S. Calvary Group moved out. In twelve hours, it had crossed the Alps and was thoroughly mixed in with British troops in northern Italy. Gen. Mark Clark, that area's commander, who had not been informed of such a movement, made haste to congratulate General Patton on the alacrity and boldness of it. He lost no time in informing General Eisenhower that additional troops were not needed. General Clark requested that the troops be withdrawn. They were—with the same zest and boldness. Patton exuded a certain sureness.

In September 1945, the Russians were staging a military review for all of the occupying powers and Patton was seated next to Marshal Zhukov of Russia. As the Russian tanks passed, Zhukov said to Patton, "My dear General Patton, you see that tank? It carries a cannon which can throw a shell seven miles." Patton replied, "Indeed? Well, my dear Marshal Zhukov, let me tell you this: If any of my gunners started firing at your people before they had closed to less than seven hundred yards I'd have them court-martialed for cowardice." The Russian commander was stunned into silence.

If Patton was extremely sure of himself and his ability, it was because he knew what he and his men could accomplish. He was particularly rankled when he was told to play it safe and was forced to keep the reins tight:

> In every case, practically throughout the campaign I was under wraps from the Higher Command. . . . I feel that had I been permitted to go all out, the war would have ended sooner and more lives would have been saved. Particularly I think this statement applies to the time when, early in September, we were halted, owing to the desire, or the necessity, on the part of General Eisenhower in backing Montgomery's move to the doubt that we could have gone through and on across the Rhine within ten days. This would have saved a great many thousand men.

Many managers who have been held back by their superiors can take heart. The military environment and the business environment are not that foreign to each other. Probably in reference to his frustrations, Patton said, "At the close of this war, I will remove my insignia and wristwatch. I will continue to wear my short coat so everyone can kiss my ass."

DO IT NOW

Urgency seems to be present when leadership is evident. Its absence is often marked by waste and repetition. The statement "We never have time to do it right, but we always have time to do it over" is an accepted business adage. But it's an adage that Patton wouldn't accept:

> *Do not regard what you do as only a "preparation" for doing the same thing more fully or better at some later time. Nothing is ever done twice. There is no next time. There is but one time to win a battle or a campaign and that's the first time.*

If this urgency were adopted in all facets of business, stress-induced health problems might offset any advantages. But the General had a good point, and managers should examine each major effort to assess if the timing will be kind enough to allow a second try if necessary. Also, Patton probably realized that the added effort to do something correctly the first time is usually small in comparison to redoing it later.

TACT

Patton has been portrayed as a man devoid of tact. *Blunt, profane, crass, shoots from the hip,* and a few other descriptive words would come to mind before the word *tact*. Yet many times, the General did exhibit tact and was widely admired for it. For example, he toasted the ladies at a West Point dinner in Kansas City, Missouri, April 5, 1924.

> *Good water is the greatest gift to set before a king.*
> *But who am I, that I should have the best of everything.*

Let monarchs gather round the pump and pass the dipper
    free.
Gin, whiskey, wine, and even beer are good enough for me.

In quoting the above I refer simply to the feeling of unwor-
thiness expressed and not in the horrid idea of excessive
potations, for in toasting the ladies, similar feelings of un-
worthiness oppress me.

Had I been called upon to toast horseflesh or profanity, or
some other subject on which I may possess erudition, I
would have been less abashed. As it is, the timorous mod-
esty of my nature and my well-known celibate instinct are
compounded. I am at a loss.

I might raise my glass to those generous-spirited ladies of
the Paris boulevards; but abstain out of regard for the feelings of some, and from the knowledge that there are others
here better qualified to sing their praises than I. And so, in
a higher vein, I might review women (ladies, if you will),
brown, mauve, or painted; dressed or "au naturel"; but
should I do so it were a sacrilege to later offer you the toast
I shall propose. In the chapel of Leavenworth, on the mon-
ument at Riley, on the walls of Cullum Hall, are names:
names of officers dead on the field of honor; bits of marble,
slate, or bronze commemorating the fact that Lt. Willie
Jones made the choice and without ostentation or hope of
reward, did his duty even unto death. The little plaques tell
the story and fame, such as it is, and high honors from us
who know, are accorded Willie. But where is Mrs. Willie's
tablet? Such were the women who year on harrowing year
made homes for officers in these bleak western ports; such
the women who today uncomplainingly share the luxury of
containment quarters. Think of the horror of the slow tor-
ture of suspense between the night of Wounded Knee or
Chateau Thierry, and the morning at the cemetery. Think
of it and thank God for the quick mercy of the bullet.
Gentlemen, I reverently pledge you: the ladies who have
shared our lives from the Equator to the Arctic; the ladies

> *who have condoned our reverses, and inspired but to ap-*
> *plaud, our successes.*
>
> *May we live to make them happy, or and the Great Day*
> *come, so die as to make them proud. The Army women,*
> *God bless them.*

George Patton understood the importance of family in the careers of officers, and the business manager should also consider not only how his or her own spouse has contributed to success but also what the employees' families mean to their success.

SUMMARY

Patton identified leadership as something he had, but he couldn't define it and neither could anyone else, at least not in terms specific enough for clinical analysis. "We know it from what they inspire and achieve," said the General. Yet, we can look at the people he inspired—the entire Third Army and some of the enemy—and his achievements and recognize some apparently contributing elements.

An awareness of the importance of a positive reputation and the damage done by a negative image can prompt a potential leader in business to make a deliberate effort to create the good image and combat the poor image. Patton emphasized the part that motivation plays in the leadership role, and an examination of his methods can serve as a guideline to the existing or aspiring manager.

The problems often expressed in terms of "improper delegation" of responsibility can be avoided when they are understood in terms of vertical span of control.

Two-way loyalty, often forgotten by managers, and a winning attitude are part of the leadership role as is a certain boldness.

A positive image, an ability to motivate, judicial use of authority, delegating responsibility, loyalty, tact, and a winning attitude are excellent qualities of leadership that Patton exemplified. Many managers can enhance leadership potential by considering these elements. The simple awareness of the importance of leadership can assist today's manager, not by answering any questions on "how to," but by asking the question, "Am I using all the elements of leadership at my disposal?" Leaders may be born and not made as are poets, but a leader can improve his odds of success by emulating one of the greatest leaders.

PATTON SAID:	A GOOD MANAGER:
☐ "Motivate positively."	☐ Motivates the employee to *want* to do, not just do.
☐ "Show confidence."	☐ Maintains a positive attitude toward the company and his job.
☐ "Play the role."	☐ Performs the manager's part in spite of problems.
☐ "Leadership is the thing that wins battles."	☐ Remains aware of the power of leadership.
☐ "A loyal officer is preferred to a brilliant one."	☐ Recognizes loyalty as a bidirectional quality.
☐ "The Army women, God bless them."	☐ Keeps in mind that others contribute significantly.
☐ "There is no next time."	☐ Attempts to do it right the first time.
☐ "Nothing is impossible. . . provided you use audacity."	☐ Avoids resisting new ideas.
☐ "Never take counsel of your fears."	☐ Commits to the task of managing.
☐ "Great disappointments are the road to success."	☐ Uses creativity to turn a liability into an asset.
☐ "Don't command too far down."	☐ Uses care in delegating authority.
☐ "This is my war face."	☐ Builds a positive image.

Chapter 4
MORALE

In Cold Weather, Officers Must Not Appear to Dress More Warmly Than the Men

My theory is that an army commander does what is necessary to accomplish his mission, and that nearly eighty percent of his mission is to arouse morale in his men.

The attitude that people have toward their jobs is only one way to describe the elusive factor of morale in business or in any organized concerted effort. In sports, morale is thought of as one of the most important contributors to a winning game and a winning season. Players are replaced for contributing to poor morale, and as soon as the teams take the field, court, or ice, either good or poor morale is noticeable. Sportwriters use the term often in their Monday morning reviews and everybody seems to know what it means. It can be measured in sports contests, to some degree, by the final score or can be evidenced by some heroic feats during the game. Whole teams have been moved from one city to another—and hundreds of millions of dollars spent—in hopes of finding an environment that will enhance team morale.

The military considers morale an important factor in the efficiency of the troops, and usually assigns an officer to constantly evaluate, as best he can, the morale of the troops. *Esprit de corps* can be defined as the animating spirit of a collective body—the soul of the organization. In management, morale seldom surfaces as something to be handled in a deliberate manner. Occasionally, it is mentioned in passing, usually by someone in the personnel department, or it is cited in a companywide memo from the president or in the annual stockholders report.

The importance of morale in a business organization is much more difficult to assess than in a sports contest. After each game, the score is posted and an assumption can be made about which team possessed it. Business does not enjoy the same timely milestones of measurement, and sometimes the lack of morale is cited only on the courthouse steps during a bankruptcy sale.

Should the morale of a management team producing and selling a product be as important as the morale of a baseball team in winning a game? There would seem to be no question.

Patton, as did most leaders, considered morale a cornerstone to success. Morale is the thing that gets people to *want* to do what you want them to do. Patton said:

> *My theory is that an army commander does what is necessary to accomplish his mission, and that nearly eighty percent of his mission is to arouse morale in his men.*

If the General's 80 percent estimate is valid, and if the missions of management are comparable in concept to the military, then perhaps our present efforts in this direction should be reevaluated. After all, both military and management have goals, objectives, people, plans, and the desire to win. Eighty percent is a big number.

Patton aroused morale in his men by showing an interest in them, by being a visible leader, by praising his men, by appealing to the men's pride, by showing an excellent example, by treating them fairly, and by communicating well. If 80 percent of a business success also concerns employee morale, and is recognized as such, then it would seem that the title "vice president for morale" should appear on the organization chart of most companies. A corporate plan to arouse morale would also seem to be appropriate. It would be interesting to develop a questionnaire that would give some indication of the morale of an organization, using as its guidelines the methods Patton relied on. The results would have to be filtered carefully and a certain measure of subjectivity would remain.

Still, the management of the company being surveyed could gain important insight into the level of morale in its organization.

INTEREST IN THE EMPLOYEE

Patton observed that it was imperative for an officer to take an interest in his men:

> *All officers . . . must be vitally interested in everything that interests the soldier. Usually, you will gain a great deal of knowledge by being interested, but, even if you do not, the fact that you appear interested has a very high morale influence in the soldier.*

Often, in business or any profession, management personnel closet themselves in the relative security of their offices and "speak only to the Lowells." Apartheid need not be racial nor strictly South African. It can be, and is, noticeable in some companies. A wall of prejudice is erected and sides are chosen. The senior design engineer refused the suggestions of the draftsman because the draftsman is an hourly paid employee and not a "professional"; the accountant condescendingly looks at the account clerk's task as demeaning and insignificant; the boss views the secretary as a typing machine incapable of contributing thought; and managers, with their assigned parking, separate dining areas, and other perks, communicate with their own level and above all exhibit an attitude of disinterest in the "troops." Often, in this atmosphere departmental bias is stirred in: The programming, department does only those things that benefit programming, engineering blames programming for everything, and manufacturing competes with every other department. Now, the so-called concerted effort becomes, in reality, a kaleidoscopic array that inhibits progress, plans, and success. The time and effort consumed in these interdepartmental squabbles can be substantial, and they can establish significant and long-lasting impediments to profitable operations. In some instances, one department may deliberately subvert the efforts of another to satisfy petty jealousies.

The success of a manager depends, to a great extent, on the ability and enthusiasm displayed by his employees. They are his most important resource, and although many managers may object, the employees are the only ones who know what is really going on in the organization. The manager, like the unsuspecting wife, is always the last to know.

LISTENING TO EMPLOYEES

Listening entails a deliberate effort on the part of some managers; to others it is entirely natural. Each employee wants to feel a part of a group—the company—and needs recognition. This does not mean that the manager has to solicit a recital of personal problems from each of his employees on a daily basis. What it does mean is that the manager should allocate some time to each employee either on a periodic basis or on an as-required basis; this interaction, however, should not be in the form of a time-phased appraisal setting, but in a friendly, helpful atmosphere. The exchange should concern the employee's job, his goals, his suggestion for improvement, and perhaps his hobbies. The manager may also choose to touch on the employee's personal life, but only if they're well acquainted. The exchange should be more in a listening mode than in a counseling mode, although counseling should be available, if requested. It's an important technique because the employee needs a time to talk about his job, and the manager can gain valuable practice in listening and perhaps gain some good information as well.

VISIBILITY

Few can be motivated by an unseen human force. The closed door and the mysterious aura of the carpeted sanctuary may, at first, inspire trepidation and awe. Normally the mystique erodes quickly and is replaced with an attitude of indifference or even worse, resentment. Any type of motivation wanes, but it doesn't take much to reestablish it. Even the divines have and had symbols, paintings, statues or some other visible signs of presence and interest. People want to see their leader. Politicians' use of television will attest to that. Patton placed a great deal of importance on visibility as an element of morale:

> *Corps and army commanders must make it a point to be*
> *physically seen by as many individuals of their command*
> *as possible. . . .*

Patton thought that the best way to do this was to assemble the units and make a short talk. If there was some danger involved, he believed the value of visibility was enhanced. At Saarlautern, on the breakthrough to the Rhine, Patton crossed a bridge under enemy fire and explained that it was purely a motion on his part to show soldiers that generals could get shot at. He was often criticized for his continued exposure to fire at the front lines, but he said, "What damn good is a general who won't take the same risks as his troops? You can't push a piece of wet spaghetti from behind." He could not tolerate a leader who was not in the forefront. One time, he came upon a column of weapons and men on a main road, completely motionless because an artillery piece was jammed beneath a rail overpass. This position put the column in severe jeopardy and exposure to air attack as well as artillery barrages. The officer in charge was halfway back in the column trying to direct his men. Patton offered the officer certain tactical alternates he could take. "Colonel," he said, "you can blow up the goddamn gun, you can blow up the goddamn bridge, or you can blow out your goddamn brains, and I don't care which."

Sometimes in management, visibility is restricted to the good times, when all decisions are of a happy type and the organization outlook is one of optimism. When the dark days come and difficult or unpleasant decisions are required, then silence, delegation, or the memo is used.

An out-of-town business trip or an important managerial seminar will allow managers to bypass the unpleasant nature of bad news. Some executives have hired consultants to stage a study with an obvious study result so that the onus of the distasteful action can be transferred to the consultant.

Yet these are the instances when visibility can do more to prop up a sagging morale than at any other time. It is relatively easy to maintain or increase morale during prosperity. When prosperity is threatened, everyone needs an uplift—or the facts—so they can plan or cope with their personal objectives.

Visibility should not be in the form of a pompous walk-through. The company president with a retinue of vice presidents making the quarterly factory visitation, at a pace close to Olympic records, hardly instills morale in the factory workers. Nor does the manager who each morning presumptuously inspects the products and criticizes loudly when faults are found. Employees need a feeling of importance and continued reassurance that the jobs they are doing have value and need doing. If the manager gets constructively involved with their jobs, even in a small way, the import of the jobs to the employees must increase. The visibility need not consume an inordinate amount of time, but if Patton were correct about the importance of instilling morale, a substantial amount of time can be expended without a bit of waste.

Inertia plays an important part in both physics and management, and it seems that the higher the level of management the more inertia is present. It is too easy for managers to just sit still and have everything brought to them.

The director of engineering calls a staff meeting: The manager of R&D reports on progress for the week; the manager of product development, with the aid of charts and graphs, explains away the budget overrun and behind-schedule condition. Each manager reports, receives direction, and returns to work. The director has yielded to inertia and has never left the office. The planning and control functions have been satisfied to some extent, but what about the function of motivation? As far as the rest of the engineering department employees are concerned, the director could stay in bed each morning and accomplish the same things via telephone.

Managers have got to overcome management inertia by getting up from their padded chairs (a major cause of "waffle ass" as Patton put it) and getting out with the people. The people need them, and the exercise won't do them any harm either.

Patton was very careful to avoid unnecessary actions that could be mistaken or misinterpreted by the troops. He advised that commanders should drive or walk up to the front and be seen by all but never be seen leaving the front and returning to the rear. "Fly back," he said. That way, the impression was left that the leader was "up there" somewhere, open to the same peril as his troops. It also helped to create a sense of unity. "He is our leader," the troops would think. "He is one of us."

Such visibility can also result in hero worship, and most of us need heroes. We were nurtured in a time of heroes whom we adopted from figures, generals, politicians, industrial magnates, gangsters, or spies. Heavy feedings from textbooks, coaches, parents, best-sellers, TV, films, and professors, to name only a few, reinforced the need. If a leader were seen driving from the battle, he would not remain a hero for long. "That SOB took one look and is now returning to the safety and comfort of his rear-echelon office," the troops would grumble. Though they know that the commander must return to his headquarters to perform his duties, they don't want to see him leave while they must remain. That's just human nature.

IN BAD TIMES

The application that this concept has to management is not far-fetched. When organizational problems occur, that is, when tensions mount and when anger flares, visibility becomes very important. Some managers seek the refuge of their offices for a series of "important meetings," while others select the alternative of a brief vacation until things settle down. To maintain or increase morale, the manager has to become visible. He may not have to stay visible, but he can't be seen running for cover.

When Patton landed in North Africa, the boats were not being pushed off the beach after unloading. The beach was under heavy shellfire, and French aviators were strafing the beach. Regardless, Patton leaped into the water and put his shoulder to the boats to help the men push them off; he stayed there for eighteen hours, completely soaked through. He quieted the nerves of the troops by not taking cover when enemy planes came over.

Another instance occurred in Messina and was reported by an officer who was under heavy German fire for many days:

> *Suddenly, I see coming in our direction up the road a cloud of dust, and damned if it isn't Patton in that open command car of his, accompanied by outriders and staff. He stops, steps down into the road and looks around as if he were looking for a seat at a baseball game. Then, almost as if on a parade ground, he started striding up the ravine toward my position where I'm sitting sweating in clothes I haven't changed in eleven days. Shells are still dropping all over the place, but they didn't seem to bother him. Anyway, he said to me, "Goddammit, colonel, get a move on, get off your behind. We've got a war to fight." Then he went and did the same to the other commanders, and a little later, I had to talk with some of the other boys and one of them summed it up. "That old son-of-a-bitch is going to get some of us killed." He did, but he got his army moving.*

Employees are like troops; they need their hero most when discouragement is present or potential.

PRAISING EMPLOYEES

Reward in the form of "atta boy" has become a trite expression in business. Yet, the reason it's so common is because it's effective. Salary is important, but several studies have indicated that job satisfaction also affects morale. The studies differ in degree of importance they attribute to each, but the consensus indicates that job satisfaction warrants more consideration. Recognition in the form of praise from a superior is a large part of job satisfaction. It satisfies the need of fulfillment and self-realization. The use of praise is hardly a management breakthrough. It has been used as a motivator since the beginning of recorded history, and most likely before. Patton used it liberally but not indiscriminately. He was not above "gilding the lily" occasionally and giving credit even when it wasn't due:

> *A general officer who will invariably assume the responsi-*
> *bility for failure, whether he deserves it or not, and invar-*
> *iably gives the credit for success to others, whether they*
> *deserve it or not, will achieve outstanding success.*

Imagine what would happen in the company environment if the General's observation became an accepted management attitude and procedure. High morale would be guaranteed, people would be lining up to become employees, productivity would have to be enhanced and profitability would result. But this is really a big concession to human nature. It is against human nature to do it. To acknowledge responsibility for failure even when we have been charged with the responsibility is difficult. But to accept it when the fault rightfully belongs to someone else is almost too much to expect. Conversely, to receive credit for success, whether or not it is deserved, is something few people would object to. For some reason, even when it's not deserved, most people will gratefully accept credit when it's given.

The positive motivation that a manager can glean from his employees and associates by this "bigness" is as much a guarantee of success as exists. Patton showed this "bigness" on several occasions. After assigning difficult tasks to his subordinates he would tell them, "Remember, I ordered you to do it. So if anything goes wrong, I'll take the blame." And this he did. For most business managers—and most human beings for that matter—this practice will entail a conscious effort.

Obviously, when managers assign difficult or potentially calamitous tasks to employees, they should not offer to assume all of the blame for everything. That attitude could promote recklessness and noninvolvement. They should offer to assume the blame of the outcome only if the task was completed judiciously but nevertheless resulted in calamity.

EMPLOYEES' PRIDE

In a recital of the seven deadly sins, pride is usually mentioned first. It didn't get to first place because of random selection. It is a proven motivator. Wars were waged over it, homicides committed because of it, and huge empires developed as an appeasement to it. Excessive pride is the substance of many TV programs and supermarket scandal sheets. A severe lack of pride provides a substantial income for many psychologists and psychiatrists. We all have some of it in varying degrees.

Although an ethical analysis of "pride" is beyond the scope of this book, its potential and effectiveness as a driving force is not. Certainly, all pride is not immoral.

Self-respect, esprit de corps. patriotic spirit and honor are all positive virtues that stem from pride. Patton worked hard to hone this tool of motivation to a sharp edge. If it motivated him, why shouldn't it motivate others?

> *Once in Sicily, I told a general, who was somewhat reluctant to attack, that I had perfect confidence in him, and to show it, I was going home. I tried the same thing that day and it worked again.*

He didn't spend much time dissecting the theory of why pride motivates people; he just knew it did. Nor did he try to technique the approach by attempting to quantify and classify its elements. He was quite satisfied that it was effective in the past and therefore the odds were that it would be effective again:

> *The weather was so bad that I gave General Eddy permission to stop the attack, which immediately induced him to attack more vigorously. Such is the nature of man.*

"Such is the nature of man." Yes, Patton knew the nature of man—strengths and weaknesses. He had both. He used both.

It is paradoxical that the manager reacts so positively to an appeal to pride, yet uses this inexpensive device as though it were on a scanty annual allotment. It appears that the flashy, hard-to-understand, impossible-to-measure-and-pronounce new management techniques of motivation are far more revered than proven standards in developing morale.

The avant-garde of motivation captured the fancy of management in the late sixties and early seventies when sensitivity training was introduced to business and gobbled up by large and small companies alike. It was a psychological Disneyland. The decision process used by many managers to justify the expenditure of a "T Training" seminar was quite different from what was normally followed. Neither cost-benefit analyses nor return-on-investment studies were performed. So why did management buy so readily? Pride, of course. Managers do not want to perceived as negative, and everyone wants to be the first kid on the block to try something new. Newness counts. Effectiveness? Well, if it happens to be effective also, all the better.

A manager should know each employee, and part of this knowledge concerns the specific actions and accomplishments of which an employee is proud. It doesn't take seven hours of therapy with the employee or an advanced degree in psychology. All the manager has to do is listen. The employee will be quite happy to share this insight with the manager or for that matter anyone else within earshot. Such is the nature of man.

The cost of using pride to improve morale is small. A little time, a little reflection, and a conscious deliberate effort are all that's required. The value of pride as a motivator is easily ascertained. When the typical soldier is asked about his outfit, he invariably answers by stating his regiment or by stating his division. "I'm with the 355th Infantry" or "I'm with the eighty-second." This practice was absent in Patton's Third Army. When asked, Patton's soldiers would always answer proudly and succinctly, "I'm with Patton." Now that's morale.

Every library has several books relating the success of pride as a motivator. They are catalogued under "History."

LEADING BY EXAMPLE

Examples of math, medicine, management, music and miscellaneous are used to portray the "right" way of doing things. To instruct, to clarify, to aid the learning process, and to emphasize importance, are their basic functions. They are also used to motivate and to de-motivate. "Provide a good example for the child," many doting grandparents have warned their children. Teachers use the example as a prime element of their lesson plans without examples, and little league coaches would all be institution-alized if they couldn't use examples. "Hold the bat like this. Grip the ball this way."

The example displayed becomes the standard of performance, good or bad. General Patton's belief in example as a motivator is legendary to those who followed him. He always had the lead and would not ask his men to do anything that he couldn't do himself. His uniform, his bearing, his personal habits, his attitude, and even his language were models for the soldiers who served with him. He was a "follow me" general.

It appears, however, that business has been somewhat less successful in providing excellent examples. "Follow me" are not the two most com-mon words heard echoing through the halls of management. All too often the examples provided by management are more prominent in providing methods to spread responsibility and evade accountability for potentially adverse effects. Tried and true techniques cover the spectrum from the cover-up memos to the voluminous "Don't Blame Me" files. More time is spent "protecting" than "doing" and this can be shown by the quantity of paperwork that is presented during the discovery process of a civil trial brought by one large company against another. Of course, the lawyers are happy and are often blamed for the tons of paperwork, but, they didn't create it—company management did.

Patton realized the waste and futility of this practice and offered ad-vice:

> Avoid as you would perdition issuing cover-up orders, or-
> ders for the record. This simply shows lack of intestinal
> fortitude on the part of the officer signing the orders, and
> everyone who reads them realizes it at once.

We are well-reminded by Watergate and Irangate that Patton's admoni-tion applies to political endeavors. It also applies to business, where cover-up memos are hardly isolated occurrences. Unhappily, employees are always the first to notice this form of sham. The cover-up memo does not contribute to increased employee morale.

Pointing the finger at procedure manuals and "higher management" has received blame for more unpleasant actions than Mrs. O'Leary's cow. They have proved to be very effective scapegoats. They allow a manager to transfer responsibility for a distasteful task. A procedure is an inanimate object and "upper management" is far removed from the average employee. When refusing an employee's request for such things as time-off, compensatory time, vacation changes, and merit increases, the manager can usually find a procedure that could be interpreted as prohibiting the action. In criticizing an employee or an organization, "policy" can be cited as the source. By using these techniques, the manager can retain the friendship of the requesting or criticized employee and the employee's wrath is transferred to the procedure or to higher management. Sometimes it works. But Patton disagreed with the practice:

> *Avoid the vicious habit of naming the next superior as the author of any adverse criticism while claiming all complimentary remarks for yourself.*

Passing the buck and grandstanding do not improve morale. Buck-passing may, for a brief period, satisfy an employee, but what is needed and sorely lacking is for the manager to set a good example. All this promotes instead is mediocrity, and mediocrity does not provide much motivation.

Compliments from a level of management higher than the manager are far more important to the employee than compliments from the manager. The words, "The president thinks you're doing a great job," said by a manager to an employee will evoke reactions similar to the words "You've won the lottery." If the declaration is made in the presence of other employees, the effect will be increased substantially. The employee's frustrations, which are part of any job, are for a time eliminated.

Another accepted practice in organizations that Patton would disagree with is for the senior manager to call the junior manager to his office for discussion. The assumption is that the time of the senior manager is more valuable than the time of the junior. "Tell Smith that I want to see him in my office," is the common statement to initiate discourse. Or, "Set up a staff meeting in my office at 3:00 P.M." Patton suggested that the senior officer visit the junior officer:

> *The more senior the officer, the more time he has. Therefore the senior should go forward to visit the junior rather than call the junior back to see him.*

This concept has seldom, if ever, been advanced at business schools, management seminars, books on management; nor has it been promoted by many literary businessmen and consultants. The belief that the senior manager has more time to spare than the junior manager will bring strong protests from incompetent or disorganized senior managers. Patton's reasoning, however, is sound because the example that would be set and the visibility that is inherent is such a practice would definitely assist in raising the morale of the troops.

Patton used the same simple logic for office layout, and even telephone answering techniques. Telephone companies advocate that managers answer their own telephones to save time for both parties. Patton agreed:

> *In my opinion, generals should answer their own phones. . . . This is not particularly wearisome because few people call a general except in emergencies, and then they like to get him at once.*

Some major company presidents already subscribe to this practice, but there are circumstances that would limit the use of this technique. If the company has attained notoriety or is the object of public scrutiny, perhaps an intermediary should be used. But, where feasible, the manager who answers his own telephone not only saves time and money but also dispels the concept of superiority that is implicit in having a secretary screen all calls. Employees feel more like members of a team when managers act as employers do. Even the president of a company is a company employee.

Current management protocol would draw plenty of criticism from the General. His ideas would at first seem sophomoric, but analysis would reveal a simple logic, difficult to refute. His methods would eliminate some of the executive trappings, but they would save time and money, and definitely increase morale.

FAIRNESS

The idea of fair play is part of the American ethic, whether one is referring to sports, school, home, or children's arguments. "Why don't you pick on someone your own size?" is a question posed by every generation that is a constant reminder of our innate desire for fairness. America is the Mecca for the underdog. America was built by underdogs. To forget this desire and exhibit unfairness will create the same indignation as giving the "favorite" a six-point handicap. Unfairness is the basic element of a morale problem.

Patton demanded that his subordinates punish everyone equally for the same crime. Often, in business, the manager can modify the punishment according to his bias. If a tool-crib employee steals a wrench, he is fired. If a manager "borrows" an expensive piece of office equipment, he is asked to return it and is reprimanded. The crime in both cases is stealing. When the punishment does not fit the crime or when two levels of equality in punishment exist, employee morale will suffer.

Patton was aware of the soldier's desire for fairness and tried to avert actions that would seem unnecessarily unfair:

> *In cold weather, general officers must be careful not to appear to dress more warmly than the men.*

He adhered to his own advice. One time he was driving in an open command car during an icy drizzle when he noticed that his driver was turning a light shade of blue. He asked the driver if he had a warm sweater and the driver replied, "No sir!" The General unbuttoned his Eisenhower jacket, peeled his sweater over his head and handed it to the driver. "Well, corporal," said Patton, "you have one now." It was a typical Patton action.

A policy of fairness can be easily transferred to business. It requires, above all, a certain sensitivity to how managerial actions are perceived by the employees. The manager took a long lunch period, even though a knotty business problem occupied the time; the manager arrived late Monday morning after a business-filled weekend. These and many others of that ilk may be justifiable, but to the employees it appears as if special liberties are being taken. The employees are unaware of the nature of the luncheon discussions and the work that occupied the weekend. What they see is what they believe—an unfair use of position. The manager should either communicate the facts to the employees or avoid the situations. Justifying one's actions to a superior or to oneself will not offset the negative effect on morale.

The manager should develop a keen degree of empathy for these instances and ask himself, "If I saw my manager taking apparent liberties and did not know the circumstances, would I be upset? Would I think that I should have the same liberties?" The answers will teach the manager how to proceed.

Patton's belief in fair play cropped up again when he was delivering the surrender terms to General Nogues, commander in chief of the French forces in North Africa. The U.S. Government had designed a long and detailed set of terms for the French general to sign. Patton thought they were unfair and humiliating. He tore up these papers in front of Nogues and said, "If you will give me your hand and your word that there will be no trouble between your people and mine, this will be surrender terms enough." It was, and the pledge was not broken.

SUMMARY

Morale can't be fractioned into identifiable parts that will all add up to 100 percent, but many of its elements can be isolated and profitably discussed. Showing an interest in each employee and listening to employees are essential to creating good morale and do not have to consume a great amount of time. Being a visual manager can have beneficial "pride-effects" by improving self-confidence and increasing leadership potential. Also, managers will probably learn quite a bit about their operations. Praising employees and giving credit in some circumstances can be difficult, but managers must consider the effects it will have on morale.

Telling an employee that a certain job is too tough will affect that person's pride and motivate the employee to succeed.

Managers who set bad examples can destroy organizational morale in a hurry. All managers should consciously strive to set positive examples. One effective way to do this is by being fair in everyday dealings with employees, especially since instances of unfairness will not be forgiven easily by subordinates.

Patton's vision for improving morale should become an agenda item at group communication meetings, and kept in the foreground of managerial discussion. Investing more time in any of the morale factors is an excellent investment. There is no downside risk.

PATTON SAID:	A GOOD MANAGER:
☐ "80% of the mission is to arouse morale."	☐ Has a deliberate plan to motivate his employees.
☐ "Be interested in the soldiers."	☐ Talks to and with his employees often.
☐ "Be seen."	☐ Doesn't hide in his office or conference room.

PATTON SAID:	A GOOD MANAGER:
☐ "Assume responsibility for failure."	☐ Doesn't use an employee as a scapegoat.
☐ "Give credit for success to others."	☐ Lets employees take the glory.
☐ "Avoid issuing cover-up orders."	☐ Learns from history's cover-ups, such as Watergate.
☐ "Avoid naming a higher authority as source of criticism."	☐ Tells it like it is, whether good or bad.
☐ "Don't claim complimentary remarks for yourself."	☐ Passes on praise from a higher level directly to the employee involved.
☐ "Go to the junior."	☐ Doesn't order the employee to come to his or her office as a rule.
☐ "Answer your own phone."	☐ Doesn't have a secretary conduct a third-degree examination of callers.
☐ "Be fair."	☐ Does unto others . . .
☐ "Be an example."	☐ Offers a model of a management executive.

Chapter 5
TEAMWORK

Let Everyone Know What They Are Supposed to Do and Why

George S. Patton is merely a hook on which to hang the Third Army.

Sports offer excellent and highly visible examples of teamwork. The fast break in basketball combines fluid speed, split-second timing, strength, an uncanny awareness of the defenders' presence, excellent hand-eye co-ordination, and a few other things that a computer would be hard pressed to duplicate. In hockey one player passing the puck while skating rapidly to a position at the other side of the ice rink while evading opposing players and their maiming attempts exhibits similar tasks. A short-to sec-ond-to first double play in baseball is teamwork exemplified as is a scram-bling quarterback throwing a 60-yard pass on the run to a teammate with outstretched arms also on the dead run. What do they all have in com-mon? Something that Patton taught his officers: "Let everyone know what they are supposed to do and why." The athletes all know what they are supposed to do, and do it well. If they are professionals, the "why" they do it for is money and fame; if they are amateurs, they do it for love of the sport.

How do they know what to do? The coach or manager has explained it to them many times, and they have practiced doing it many times. If they don't follow the coach's instructions they are disciplined. Why is teamwork so important in sports? Because without it, the team would function as individuals without a sense of unity and purpose. It's as simple as that.

General Patton built teamwork because a military unit without it does not win battles or wars. His Third Army, composed of many corps and divisions, was his company, and the soldier identified with the army organization rather than a divisional or corps organization within the army. "I'm with Patton," they said proudly.

Patton always stressed that no one man can conduct an army, and the success of an army depends on the harmonious working of its staff and the magnificent ability of its officers and enlisted men. "Without this teamwork, war cannot be successfully fought." Patton, of course, was not the first to recognize the importance of teamwork. The concept is high on every personnel manager's list of things to be stressed. "Develop teamwork," appears so often on job plans that it might as well be included in the printed format of the job plan form. Sometimes it seems that everyone is teaching it, promoting it, and blaming failure on the lack of it. But how many are really practicing it? Patton did. And he wouldn't tolerate anyone who worked against it:

> *Staff officers of inharmonious disposition, irrespective of their ability, must be removed. A staff cannot function properly unless it is a united family.*

The "united family" is a team, and the success or failure of a plan is directly related to how well that team functions as a unit. Management is often reluctant to "remove" team members by termination, and because of this reluctance team results are severely limited. If all team members except one are committed to a specific direction and that one is either uncommitted or opposed, the odds on reaching the goal get a lot slimmer.

Patton often used football examples to emphasize his concern for teamwork and the difficulty in winning games without it. Coach Woody Hayes, the legendary football coach of Ohio State who turned out more all-Americans and sent more players into the pro ranks than any other coach in history, used to use Patton's actions as examples. Hayes revered Patton as his hero of heroes, and he knew every facet of the General's campaigns and philosophy.

One of the finest examples of teamwork in history occurred not in a Super Bowl but at Bastogne during World War II. The Battle of the Bulge was, perhaps, the most publicized of all actions during the war. Elements of the American First Army were encircled and trapped at Bastogne. On December 19, 1944, Patton informed Ike that he could attack the enemy at Bastogne on December 23 with three divisions that had just come off the combat line. Eisenhower and his General Staff thought that it was totally impossible to move three battle-weary divisions a distance of 125 miles over snow-covered icy roads in absolutely miserable winter weather and engage the enemy, all within four days. Patton finally won his argument and was allowed to try to relieve the troops at Bastogne. Upon receipt of the permission, Patton telephoned his deputy, General Gay, spoke a single code word, and three divisions were on their way. Patton did not attack on December 23 as he had promised—he attacked on December 22.

The ahead-of-schedule feat may seem impressive in itself, but to realize the full extent of the effort, the details of the operation must be examined. During those few days Patton moved approximately 50,000 men, more than 1,000 large guns, 13,000 vehicles, and 62 tons of supplies a distance of more than 100 miles. The vehicles drove a total of 1 million miles, and 20,000 miles of communication wires were laid. All of this was done in inclement weather. Whatever classroom definition is assigned to teamwork, it is probably lacking in comparison to what Patton accomplished.

How did Patton accomplish such a Herculean feat? Teamwork. Each soldier knew what he was supposed to do and did it. It is interesting to note that Generals Bradley and Hodges both received Distinguished Service Medals for their unsuccessful defense of the Bulge. Patton received nothing for successfully defending it.

Can teamwork concepts from sports and the military be transferred to management? Certainly, but with some minor differences. In the late 1960s and all during the 1970s, "teamwork" became a management buzzword and many psychologists smiled, rubbed their hands in glee, and became industrial psychologists and teambuilding specialists. For $10,000 they would take an organizational group of about twenty people to an isolated seminar facility and teach the group in three days how to build a team. To impress the participants, they would conduct sessions into the evenings. It was termed team building sensitivity training, or organizational development, and employed several psychological games and devices with the advertised purpose to develop interpersonal relationships so that everybody could coexist happily, or at least politely.

What the psychologists generally forgot was that the purpose of teamwork was a desired output. The quarterback doesn't have to like the personality of the receiver. It helps, but as long as he can put the ball in the hands of the receiver after a long graceful arc, he's doing his job. The second baseman does not have to be pals with the first baseman to turn a double play. It's the output that counts.

Some small companies and a few large companies have displayed teamwork impressively. The Boeing Company is an example. Generally, the employees identify themselves with the company rather than a division of the company. Teamwork concepts are instilled there by management.

The average company, sad to say, seems to lack any high degree of teamwork and the reasons for the lack may be quite numerous. The manager or coach in the business field may not know what to do, how to do it, or why it should be done. If the manager doesn't know, then it will be impossible to explain to the team of employees, who can't practice what they don't know. The manager is really saying to the employees, "Go skate around the ice for a while." Perhaps by accident or divine intervention, they will form up into a team.

Another reason could be that the manager just doesn't care whether they win or lose since any loss can be blamed on other managers. It could be that the manager knows what to do but just can't explain it adequately to the employees. With effort, those conditions can be corrected, but there is another possible reason, which is that the employees do not want to learn their jobs. In that instance, replacement seems to offer the only alternate.

REORGANIZATIONS

The Wall Street Journal, Forbes, and other business periodicals continually report on newly appointed managers, directors, and presidents with frequent follow-up articles describing "major reorganizations" initiated by the newly appointed individual. In fact, it's almost expected. There is a penchant for a new manager to initiate some violent changes in the organization to prove to the onlookers and especially those who selected him that he is indeed a dynamic manager. The theory here is, "If they didn't want changes, they would have kept my predecessor." On a losing hockey team, there may be some logic to immediately changing the formation of the front line, but a good coach will never change the composition of a winning line.

A new manager should observe how the present organization is reacting to the current business winds and compare the reaction to some referenced standard. Then, if drastic action were required, the manager can explain the action in logical terms. The length of time would certainly depend on the size, type, substance, and circumstances of the organization, but Patton thought that a new commander should avoid rash or quick decisions:

> *Look Before Changing: In the old navy of sail there was a custom that the new officer of the deck did not call for any change in the setting of the sails for one half hour. The same thing might well apply to commanders who take over new jobs. They should wait a week before they make any radical changes. . . .*

The new manager may discover, while he is testing the water, new and current information that will lead to minor team readjustment that will in turn have a synergistic effect on the organization's output. The minor adjustment could improve productivity noticeably without personnel traumas and morale problems. The lack of violent management upheaval coupled with the improved productivity using the same resources will give the manager better visibility to higher management. If, however, a major change is necessitated, the manager will have lost relatively little by waiting and will have gained the confidence of the employees.

Reorganization in business is not a twentieth century design. In A.D. 66, Petronius Arbiter, deputy controller to Nero, observed a business phenomenon that has reoccurred down through the centuries. He related it for posterity:

> *We trained hard . . . but it seemed that every time we were beginning to form up into teams, we would be reorganized. I was to learn later in life that we tend to meet any new situation by reorganizing . . . and a wonderful method it can be for creating the illusion of progress while producing confusion, inefficiency, and demoralization.*

Petronius realized a long time ago that reorganization is not the answer to all business problems and he did not even occupy himself fully with business. (He was also the Hugh Hefner of the toga set.)

REMOVING DEADWOOD

Since all improvement requires change, many believe that all changes constitute improvement and use change as a vehicle to fire employees. Those employees who do not offer homage to the new leader, who do not appear to excel at their jobs, and some who quietly apply themselves are in jeopardy as a reorganization occurs. "Just getting rid of the deadwood," they claim. But often, much of the so-called deadwood can be shaped to perform extremely important functions. Of course, someone has to take the time to shape it. Good managers are careful not to get rid of deadwood before they have tried to ascertain whether the deadwood consists of employees who have refused to learn or just employees who have never been trained.

At one time, Eisenhower assigned a marginal general to Patton's staff, and Patton complained bitterly to Ike about the general's incompetence. Ike overruled and later when the same general blundered badly, Ike told Patton he was right and they would have to get rid of him. Patton objected and when Ike reminded Patton that it was Patton's original idea to get rid of him, Patton replied, "He was one of your spare generals then. Now he's one of my generals. I'll straighten him out myself."

Some business managers contend that deadwood can be transformed into productive employees simply by expanding the concepts and principles of teamwork.

POSITIONING TEAMWORK

Teamwork can only be effective in companies or organizations that believe in planning, because without a plan to execute, it is difficult to assign objectives to the team if the team doesn't clearly understand the things it has to do and why it does them. Members will wander aimlessly, performing perfunctory tasks and trying to look productively occupied. Teamwork should start in the boss's office and then involve each successively lower management echelon for optimum efficiency. It should result from a dictate from above rather than a conspiracy from within.

Patton lamented that while the Third Army had effective teamwork, the Allies in their overall organization did not. Had they followed his example a "great many thousand men would have been saved" and the war would have ceased months earlier than it did. Patton's army exercised excellent teamwork because he put an end to internal hostilities early on, so his organizations functioned smoothly even though the higher organization did not. The same could be said of business. Whatever level of organization introduces the concepts and practices of teamwork, the results will bring higher productivity and value to the organization's output. Teamwork that exists only in the shipping department may not have the same impact on the company that teamwork in the corporate offices would produce, nevertheless, it is worthwhile.

Taking command of a new organization and immediately removing the so-called deadwood to impress the onlookers can have a serious and potentially long-lasting ill effect. The employees remaining after the purge will be understandably concerned regarding their own future and could pull back into their shells of limited or no-risk action. The lack of forward and positive action could disable the organization far worse than the existence of temporary deadwood.

CLASS DISTINCTION

Can teamwork be effective if there is class distinction among members of the team, or must they all be of the same management level? Patton certainly was not on the level of the other team members. Rank made sure of that. But Patton's outlook was one that did not in any way reveal that the contributions of any team members were less important than his own. He was the team coach and knew that he didn't win battles by himself. In sports, several class distinctions are always present, and the team coach or manager is, in many instances, a lower-paid member of the team. The salaries of the team members differ drastically as do their backgrounds. Their salary is based upon their past and expected contributions to the teams goals and objectives, which really means the gate receipts, participation in post-season play, and their agents' finesse. In business the manager is usually not on the same level as the other team members because of the organizational structure. He is the coach and must remember that. He can't do the job himself and should not view other team members as being less important contributors. He does lead, but they produce.

PRESENT EFFORTS

"Teamwork" has a nice ring to it and, like mom and the flag, is always advocated and adored. Seminars, books, and university courses are valuable if the precepts they teach are practiced after the course. Some psychologically based courses are available, but they often fail to focus on the teamwork output.

A Japanese company offers a new type of teamwork management training that has proved to be very effective in Japan. Since 1979, 80,000 managers have been ushered through a thirteen-day grueling program that includes hazing, calisthenics, night hikes, and action debates. They attend sixteen-hour days of repetitive training in decision making, report writing, care of subordinates, and other topics. They sing songs to motivate themselves and have many badges of shame pinned to their uniforms. As they meet their instructor's standards, the badges are removed. The badges serve to remind the participants that they alone are nothing, and the good of the group is everything. It's an exciting approach to creating teamwork.

The course has been packaged for U.S. consumption, and the Japanese advocates project success in the United States because of U.S. management's awe of Japanese managerial techniques. There's a general feeling that U.S. companies are getting very soft and weak in their way of demanding excellence and, indeed, many are embracing this hell-camp type of management training at a price of $2,500 a head.

Patton would probably have disagreed with that type of training. His training methods were geared to independent thinking, not unanimity, in his officers. Also any training that included shame as a motivation would not have agreed with him. He motivated people through pride. He might, however, have approved of the physical aspects of the training since he believed that exercise and good health tend to overcome tiredness. He said, "There are more tired division and corps commanders than there are tired divisions and corps. Also, a tired commander is always pessimistic."

SUMMARY

Teamwork is a necessary and obvious component in sports, but in business, it is neither as evident nor as obviously important. businesses do survive without it, but its contribution to business success is not given the emphasis it deserves. In sports, the goals and objectives of the team are simple and obvious; those of management may be complex and hidden. The degree of success of teamwork in business depends on the definition of the goals and objectives and on assuring that all team members know what they do and why.

The manager who strives to create good teamwork functions like a good coach, and keeps the goals and objectives in perspective all the time.

In forming teamwork, sudden and rash movement in reorganizations can be dangerous to the overall good of the company. Existing deadwood should be examined for potential improvement before replacement action.

Managers would do well to consider Patton's response when he was praised:

> *This ovation is not for me, George S. Patton. George S. Patton is merely a hook on which to hang the Third Army. Now that sounds like, "what a great man George S. Patton is" but I did not have anything to do with it. The people who actually did it are the younger officers and soldiers of the Third Army.*

Like a good coach, Patton instructed his troops how to work well as a team, then they went ahead and took his advice to heart.

PATTON SAID:	A GOOD MANAGER:
☐ "Don't make changes for the sake of change."	☐ Waits to see how the current organization reacts before making changes.
☐ "He's my general now, I'll straighten him out."	☐ Develops team members into contributing players.
☐ "Harmonious team action is a must."	☐ Removes a team member who won't perform.
☐ "Without teamwork war cannot be successfully fought."	☐ Recognizes the importance of teamwork in success.
☐ "Let everyone know what they are supposed to do and why."	☐ Make sure that the employees know what their jobs are and why they are important.

Chapter 6
RECRUITING

You Are Attached to My Headquarters, to Me Personally

The soldier is the army. No army is better than its soldiers.

If one were to apply these sentiments to business, most managers would agree with the resulting statements: "The employee is the company. No company is better than its employees." And yet, although thousands upon thousands of words have been written on the care and treatment of employees, not a great deal of thought has been given to hiring practices.

The employee turnover rate can be, and often is, a barometer of employee morale, and everyone knows that employees coming and going costs money. The cost of acquiring a new employee and the cost of the period of time that the new employee is unproductive has been estimated up to $100,000 depending on the type of job. If the company were purchasing a new piece of equipment that costs $100,000, studies would be made, vendors would be surveyed, cost break-even points determined, and signatures would be required from managers at every level up through the board of directors. Yet some companies use the same techniques to recruit and hire a new employee as they do when making a minor purchase. Seldom is the hiring of a new employee allotted the time and planning commensurate with the acquisition of a valuable and costly asset.

STAFFING

Patton, even during his early career, drew to him men of rare character and unswerving loyalty. One reason he was able to do this was that he told his men what he wanted, when it was wanted, and the condition that would exist after it was done. He let them figure out how to do it. He recalled one incident in France in 1917 when he had to take over command of a newly formed First Tank Brigade and things were in a mess. He noticed a familiar-looking soldier going by and called to him. "Hey, corporal, goddammit, aren't you Thompson?" The man saluted and said, "Yes, sir, Colonel Patton. I am." "Well from now on it's Sergeant Thompson and you are attached to my headquarters, to me personally. Thompson, I've been over our equipment list and we're three touring cars and four motorcycles short." Thompson just saluted again and left on his errands. Early the next morning he reported eagerly to Patton: "The colonel will, I hope, be glad to know that he is now one touring car and two motorcycles ahead." In business, this approach might be called Results Management or Management by Objectives, but whatever it's called, it is effective.

Selecting employees is a critical function that often is carried out with more emotion than logic. A surprising number of managers hire people who agree with their politics, philosophy, and even religion. They indicate that they want people "with whom they can communicate comfortably." If "comfortable communication" is their primary function in the company, their reasoning may be suitable. But often the manager is so happy with his own image, he wants to clone himself so that he can have a group that operates in total harmony: a oneness in decision and thought. It may be ego satisfying, but it's wasteful. What he needs are people with different thoughts, modes, and experiences.

All too often the hiring process begins with a newspaper advertisement:

> *This position offers the right person an opportunity for un-*
> *limited advancement as well as a management challenge*

unique in this industry. This position reports to higher management and only those who believe in hard work need apply. Salary commensurate with experience.

Those who are unacquainted with personnel parlance may indeed be impressed, but any personnel manager can translate its true meaning. "Unlimited advancement" indicates that the pay scale for this job will probably be pretty close to the bottom, thereby leaving plenty of room to move up. "A management challenge unique in this industry" means that no one is really sure what the job entails and the new employee will have a challenge trying to discover the job functions. "Reports to higher management" simply means that the position reports to the president—through a leadman, supervisor, general supervisor, chief, manager, director, and vice president. The reference to hard work is an appeal to the Protestant work ethic and also suggests that the company is a dynamic, shirt-sleeved, gung-ho organization. "Salary commensurate with experience" can be translated to mean, "We don't know what the proper salary level for this job is, but we will pay you ten percent more than you're getting now." Sometimes the alternative "salary open" is used.

The employee requisition form generally initiates the hiring action. It is prepared by the person who wants to hire an employee. If the originator can't describe exactly what he wants, the personnel department can't be held accountable for not recruiting the perfect candidate. If the description is adequate, the hiring process should result in recruiting the best candidate at the time, not simply any candidate. That entails a great deal of work to uncover a sufficient number of candidates to interview so that the best can be selected. The Japanese are beginning to realize the importance of the hiring process, and some companies interview over 100 candidates for each open position.

Generally, the manager who initiates the employee requisition makes the final selection of the candidate. If the personnel department does not screen out the applicants who definitely do not qualify for the job, the manager tends to believe that the applicants sent in are representative of the average. The manager may mentally readjust his own requirements accordingly. The first average applicant, one who has minimum qualifications, is hired. Often it's another poor investment.

The days of psychological games in personnel departments that marked the 1960s and 1970s are, for the most part, gone. But they have left a few vestigial remnants. Some companies employ graphology as an employee selection method while at the same time jokingly comment about the use of astrology in Washington, D.C. The company that uses the pseudo-sciences such a graphology, astrology, and biorhythms instead of a manager's experience and discernment has a very serious problem. It doesn't believe in its managers. To eliminate an applicant from consideration of a job because of the juxtaposition of a couple of stars or because of the upward or downward slant of one's handwriting is not a practice Patton would have endorsed. "Does he have the qualifications to do the job and the willingness to do the job" are the questions Patton would have asked.

Beyond the obvious technical and military requirements, the General looked for a desire to win in a staff candidate. He would not select an officer who had what he called "a defensive mentality" and pointed out many times that battles and wars have never been won by defensive tactics. Defensive tactics indicate the absence of a desire to win in both the military and business environment. Criteria for selecting staff in both should include:

☐ A desire to win

☐ An ability to do the job

☐ An ability to take hard work in stride

☐ Creativity

In staff selection, Patton was blessed with having an excellent personnel department—the draft board. He had a pretty large pool from which to select, and the qualities he sought were more readily identifiable. The ability to do the job, work hard, use creativity, and a strong desire to win will be far more difficult to discern in a management applicant. Yet, the manager can, with a deliberate effort, devise interview questions that will indicate the presence of these qualities to some degree.

THE NEW EMPLOYEE

For Patton an officer's responsibility extended far beyond giving orders and expecting results:

> *Officers are responsible not only for the conduct of their men in battle but also for their health and contentment*

*when not fighting. An officer must be the last man to take
shelter from fire, and the first to move forward. Similarly,
he must be the last man to look after his own comfort at the
close of a march.*

If a manager's responsibility, in any manner, parallels Patton's concept of an officer's responsibility to his men, then much more attention should be accorded the new employees' introduction to the company. For example, what happens to the employee's spouse if the hiring requires a relocation needs to be examined. Twenty years ago concerns of this nature were minimal but now, in the age of dual-career couples, finding a job for the spouse of the new employee may be a requirement. More and more of the nation's larger companies provide some form of outside job assistance for the spouse of a new or transferred employee. Normal moving expenses are not enough. Some companies now pay for résumé writing, job counseling, and job-finding trips for spouses.

The employee's first day on the job can be a traumatic experience, but both the new employee's manager and the personnel department can buffer the trauma. Some companies will treat the arriving new employee with an air of indifference that may heighten the employee's anxiety. If made to wait, the new arrival may start to wonder: "In the letter of job offer, they made me feel that the destiny of the entire company hinged on my acceptance. Now I'm left lounging in this stark lobby for more than two hours." The attitude that the employee will develop regarding the company is affected by the first introduction to it. Care should be exercised.

Patton's advice to staff that members of his command understand what to do and why they are doing it is essential to the manager who will orient the new employee. The manager should introduce the new employee to a teamwork structure with a meaningful explanation of the new employee's duties and responsibilities and how they mesh with organizational objectives. Or the manager can, as many do, place the new employee at the desk of some other employee who is out of town and have the person read the corporate procedure manual, the division procedure manual, and the department instruction manual. This will occupy the new employee for about a week, which will give the manager more time to figure out what to do with him.

Is it any wonder that a new employee who is treated with indifference displays enthusiasm and interest with a half-life of about two weeks? By this time he knows he has been had and all the beautiful words have meant nothing.

Generally, the personnel department *is* the company to new employees or applicants. The professionalism, friendliness, and truthfulness displayed by this department will have a lasting effect on new employees. If they find that what they were originally told was entirely false, they'll grow skeptical about receiving equitable treatment in the future. Eventually their attitude may worsen and they'll become uncooperative. Thus, the return of this valuable investment will be nothing, or worse, a negative factor.

KEEPING AN EMPLOYEE

Business constantly worries about the well-being of the employee. It must, for every management magazine contains articles on "happy employees." The flexible work week, more people involvement in product production, employee councils, and quality circles are only some of the programs designed for the employee to increase morale and thereby increase profit.

The theory is excellent, but while new motivational programs are being designed and implemented, some of the old stable programs are being compromised and in some cases completely mismanaged. Much of this occurs because managers forget their function and embrace mediocrity. Patton remarked on a similar military condition:

> There is a regrettable tendency on the part of company officers and noncommissioned officers to accompany the firing lines as if they were members of a well-trained chorus, simply keeping position. This attitude of mind, and the actions resulting from it, is impossible in battle. Officers and noncommissioned officers are there for the purpose of seeing that all of the weapons of their respective little commands are functioning. They cannot see this by simply accompanying the movement; they must direct it.

The manager's job is to stay in the forefront of the organization and assure that the policies of the company as promulgated to the employees are carried out. The manager ensures that employee merit raises are used to motivate and reward exceptional performance and not merely to offset inflation.

Some personnel departments have initiated procedures that require

each organization to disperse merit funds in accordance with a performance rating of all employees in the organization; the outcome must agree
with the Gaussian curve. This Gaussian distribution arrangement necessarily has to rate some employees as below average. Patton would have
criticized any rating system that required him to rate a certain percentage
of his troops as below average. Patton thought that all his men were above
average. That's why they won all of their battles. He would claim that if
you're looking for average troops, consult the losers. Any manager who
would rate any of his employees as "below average" has not performed
the function well. If they were below average, the manager should have
taken steps to correct that condition and, if necessary, remove the employees so labeled.

Merit raises should be allocated to the manager, who should be allowed to disburse the funds as he or she sees fit. If the manager is incorrect in assigning merit raises, it will show up quickly as a morale
problem. Either the employee receiving the raise will object or the employee's fellow workers will.

Most companies require that managers hold a formal performance
evaluation with each of their employees at least once a year. Many times
the personnel evaluation forms are designed by the personnel department and require the evaluator to rate each employee on such virtues as
honesty, integrity, loyalty, communications ability, the ability to get along
with others, and the employee's ability to perform the assigned task.
These forms may then be used as the basis for merit increases.

Rating objective virtues is one of the few jobs that is beyond the managerial role. It is God's job. Managers should restrict themselves to rating
the performance toward goals, and it certainly should be done more frequently than every six months or once a year. Perhaps it should occur
weekly. If a form is necessary to assist in the evaluation it should be destroyed after the session. The more places in which personnel data are
recorded, the less truthful the data tends to be.

The employee performance evaluation, if used correctly by a committed manager, is not an employee rating at all. Like the final exam in
school that is really a yardstick of how well the teacher taught, the employee performance evaluation is, in the final analysis, how well the manager managed.

A good manager might advise his employees with Patton's own words:

> *I wish to assure all of the officers and soldiers that I never*
> *have and never will criticize them for having done too*

*much. However, I shall certainly relieve them for doing
nothing.*

SUMMARY

If the new employee is a valuable asset and represents a considerable
investment, then at least the same care and examination that is exercised
to purchase a major piece of production equipment should be used. Managers should interview many before deciding and maintain high requirement standards. They don't need clones of themselves. Instead they
should seek candidates who do something—doers. Finally, good managers will look for indications of the following:

☐ A strong desire to win

☐ An ability to do the job

☐ An ability to work hard

☐ A tendency toward creative approaches

Once the employee is hired, the person should be treated with at
least the same respect as the new piece of equipment. Managers must
remember that how the employee is handled when being introduced to
the company will contribute to a developing attitude concerning the company. The new arrival shouldn't be left in a corner to rust but be primed
on his new assignment and the teamwork structure.

As the new employee progresses, his or her merit raises if appropriate, could be viewed as maintenance costs in a productive machine.
As the oil filter ad so aptly puts it, "Pay me now, or pay me later." Patton
awarded decorations fairly liberally. As he said, "We must exploit their
abilities and satisfy their longings to the utmost. Surely, an inch of satin
for a machine gun nest put out of action is a bargain not to be lightly
passed up."

Excellent managers will remember that the employee performance
evaluation is really a self-evaluation. It should be used by every manager
as a vehicle for improved leadership methods.

These suggestions are not easily converted to reality unless a manager
wants to win *all* his battles, as Patton did, not just a few, as Montgomery
did. It's a tough decision.

PATTON SAID:	A GOOD MANAGER:
☐ "An Army is no better than its soldiers."	☐ Realizes that the company image is a reflection of the employees.
☐ "Tell them what to do and why."	☐ Introduces the new employee to teamwork concepts and practices.
☐ "Wars are not won by defensive tactics."	☐ Looks for indications that an applicant has a desire to win.
☐ "Officers look after their men first, then themselves."	☐ Treats the new employee as the manager would like to be treated.
☐ "Decorations should be used liberally."	☐ Rewards employees for excellent results.

Chapter 7
DECISION MAKING

There Is No "Approved" Solution to Any Tactical Situation

Commanding an army is not such a very absorbing task except that one must be ready at all hours of the day and night to make some momentous decisions, which frequently consist of telling somebody who thinks that he is beaten that he is not beaten.

Business decisions are rarely made with the immediacy of military decisions—nighttime business decisions are not very common—but managers must be ready to make decisions at all times. Frequently they must convince employees who think they are beaten that they're not; often they have only to convince themselves. The toughest decision managers have to make is to commit themselves to managing. After that, the decisions they have to make come fairly easy.

A decision is the willingness to risk something in making a guess about the future. The greater the consequence of failure, the greater the importance of careful consideration prior to making the decision.

Generally, there are two major classifications of decision making; revocable and irrevocable, that is, ones that can be changed rather easily and ones that can't. Stepping out of an airplane as a sky diver is an irrevocable decision; strapping on a parachute on the ground is not. Committing a crime is an irrevocable decision, as is tearing down a facility and building a new one. Military decisions are frequently irrevocable; business decisions are far less likely to be. In business, each major decision should be identified early in the decision making process so that the proper emphasis can be exercised. Irrevocable decisions deserve a second look and more in-depth investigation, time permitting of course.

POPULAR OR UNPOPULAR DECISION

Giving your employees an unexpected ten percent raise is a popular type of decision. Everybody will like you, there will be no repercussions, and morale will increase. These decisions are pleasant to make. Decisions regarding the purchase of new equipment or facilities, although possibly risky, can be successful with sufficient examination. Few will attempt to subvert your decision because it does not cause problems or effect anybody in a negative manner. The manager can expect help, cooperation, or, at worst, indifference from fellow managers.

It is the unpopular decisions that cause problems, and some come from unexpected decisions. Patton realized this because he had to make many unpopular decisions. He also realized the fortitude required to stand by the decision:

> *You must be single-minded. Drive for the one thing you have decided. You will find that you will make some people miserable; those you love and very often yourself. And, if it looks like you are getting there, all kinds of people, including some whom you thought were loyal friends will suddenly show up doing their Goddamndest, hypocritical best to trip you up, blacken you and break your spirit. Politicians are the worst; they'll wear their country's flag in public, but they'll use it to wipe their asses in the caucus room, if they think it will gain them a vote.*

In a decision, especially an unpopular one, the manager must be committed to the decision and follow through at the same time, appraising the situation for unexpected problems. Unhappily, many managers avert this problem by only making the popular decisions and blaming someone else for the unpopular ones.

The commitment to managing also eliminates vacillating each time a protest is encountered. In 1944, Patton attended one of Ike's planning meetings and at the time Patton was the army's foremost military expert on amphibious landings. He described the lack of commitment:

> *We are in the clutches of the "masterminds" here with the inevitable results that we are changing our decisions more often than we are changing our underwear. I have been consulted no more than I was when we landed in Sicily.*

The two points he brought out were that no one was committed to a given decision and the foremost expert on the subject (himself) was not asked for his opinion.

A manager should follow a deliberate process before making a decision and committing to it. In that process, the first step is to box or isolate the specific circumstances requiring the decision. This can be difficult because many situations do not exist in any insulated state. They have tentacles that seem to spread all over.

Defining why a decision has to be made in one brief statement and examining that statement for appropriateness can eliminate or reduce the probability of a poor decision. For instance, is a decision to reduce the number of employees by ten percent aimed at trimming unnecessary workers or is the purpose of the decision to reduce labor costs by ten percent? There are not too many alternatives in the first instance, but many abound in the second. In the first, ten percent of the people go out the gate. In the second, the relative merits of alternatives, such as a reduced work week, extended vacations, and reduced salaries, can be evaluated and measured for minimum adverse impact on the company.

The exact reason for the decision can be assessed on a "ladder of abstraction," which consists of a number of selected definitions that represents possible explanations. This process is used to determine the different levels of abstraction among the selected definitions. To increase the level of abstraction, the question "why" is asked. If the selected definition were "reduce personnel" the "why" would probably result in the definition "to reduce labor costs." That definition in turn prompts the query as to why labor costs have to be reduced, the answer being "to generate profits." Each time the question is asked, the answer moves into an area of greater generality. To define the reason in more specific terms, the question "how" is used. How will "reduce personnel" be accomplished? By "terminating employees." Each successive challenge of "how" provides a more specific answer. The manager should go up and down this ladder until he feels comfortable that he has viewed the proper range. In this case the ladder might be:

1. Satisfy stockholders.

2. Generate profit.

3. Reduce labor costs.

4. Reduce employee count.

5. Terminate employees.

The importance of choosing the definition that best fits the purpose can be clearly demonstrated by looking at each and recording various other methods that could be used to satisfy each. Satisfying stockholders could be accomplished by declaring a dividend or a stock split. Generating profits could be done by selling the property, investing in the stock market, increasing sales, or increasing prices. Methods of reducing labor costs have already been mentioned. When it gets down to reducing personnel, the alternatives are severely limited. Selecting an incorrect purpose can waste time and money.

This deliberate process cannot be arduously pursued for every decision a manager makes in a day. If it were, the "white coat" men would be knocking on the office door before 3 P.M. But when a decision involves a large number of dollars, people, or could have an unwanted effect of serious magnitude, it should be used. The process does not require substantial time in all cases. It can be modified to fit the circumstances, it can be done with the aid of staff members, or it can be a rapid mental exercise. Whatever time it takes is never wasted.

After the decision purpose has been defined to the satisfaction of the manager, alternative methods of satisfying the alternatives are, the more apt the manager is to bypass the mediocre ones and arrive at an outstanding decision. The techniques of creativity explained in Chapter 8, can help in developing long lists of alternatives.

The next stage is the evaluation phase where each alternative developed is evaluated in terms of adequacy. Each should be viewed not in a negative manner, but in a positive vein. Not by listing what is wrong with the alternative and why it won't work, but rather what can be added to it to make it work. Using the previous example, the manager might reject the alternative "reduce employees' salaries" as too drastic and too morale damaging. But promises of higher salaries at a future point, or the issuance of stock options, may change the alternative from negative to positive. After each alternative has been evaluated, the best choice should be implemented.

If time and conditions permit, the decision should be tested by implementing it in a manner that will indicate in a short time its validity. Previewing it with experts in that particular area is an excellent method of testing. Patton recalled one instance:

> *Ike and Clark were in conference as to what to do. Neither of them had been to the front, so they showed a great lack of decision. They have no knowledge of men or war.*

The generals desperately needed an expert—someone who had been to the front—to help in the decision process.

Once decided, the decision should be communicated to those involved with a clear definition of the intent of the decision, and a clear sense of the manager's commitment to it. The commitment must show as a strength. Patton mentioned to Ike a poor condition that existed in the high command and Ike answered, "Don't I know it, but what can I do?" Patton commented, "That is a hell of a remark for a *supreme* commander." The manager must take the responsibility and accountability for each decision.

Some managers are prone to offer so-called snap judgments that should not be discarded too hastily. If the manager has a high percentage of effective decisions, the snap judgment should be heard and considered. Patton complained:

> *For years I have been accused of making snap decisions. Honestly, this is not the case because I am a profound military student and the thoughts I express, perhaps too flippantly, are the result of years of thought and study.*

The flippant business manager may have years of experience, thought, and study behind his remarks as well.

REACTING UNDER PRESSURE

Quite a few poor decisions are those that are composed in haste, under pressure, and in the absence of ample time, proper investigation, and expert advice. When Patton selected a staff member he thought it extremely important to see how the applicant would react under pressure. In many instances he would simulate pressure circumstances to find out. Then he would apologize for the sham and explain the reasons to the officer. He worked his men hard and subscribed to the philosophy of an old friend and surgeon who believed that men do not work themselves to death, at least not real men. "What happens is that men stop looking forward, stop learning new things, and then they rust to death."

TIMING

Many serious morale problems in business are management decisions, long delayed. Timing is a critical factor in the decision-making process. If a decision is made too early—and it can be made too early—valuable time that could have been used for investigation or deliberation is wasted. If it is too late, opportunities are sacrificed.

Patton didn't believe in wasting time and didn't believe there was ever a reason for any man to be idle:

> Lack of orders is not excuse for inaction. Anything done vigorously is better than nothing done tardily.

He believed that the British army never exploited situations in a timely manner and as a result many lives were lost. He said, "We never had to regroup, which seemed to be the chief form of amusement for the British armies."

Timing has always been an important part of management operations, but the changing nature of business, especially in the technical field, now demands a new look at what have been deemed acceptable time standards for many business operations. Improved communications methods, improved data storage and retrieval systems, better-designed tools, and a host of other changes have pushed timeliness to near the top of management considerations. Things must be accomplished with dispatch.

On May 5, 1945, Major General Huebner was sitting down to dinner, about 7:30 P.M., when his aide came in with orders assigning his corps to the Third Army. General Huebner remarked, "Well, I'll give us just about twelve hours before General Patton calls up and tells us to attack something." The soup was still hot when the chief of staff of the corps was called from the table to the phone. He came back with a grin on his face, saying, "General, it's General Patton. He wants to talk with you." The conversation went something like this:

"Hello, Huebner?"

"Hello, General. How are you?"

"Fine. Where in hell have you been since Sicily?"

"Oh, we've been around making a nuisance of ourselves."

"I'm sure glad you're back with me again."

"Glad to be back, General."

"I want you to attack Pilsen in the morning."

"Yes, sir!"

"Can you do it?"

"Yes, sir."

"Fine, move fast now. We haven't got much time left in this war. I'll be up to see you. Good-bye."

"Good-bye."

General Huebner returned to the table and said, "Well, I missed that one. Instead of twelve hours, it was twelve minutes. We attack Pilsen at daybreak."

The ability to make a decision in a timely manner was a trait that Patton demanded in his staff. One general who could not make timely decisions was soon relieved by Patton of command. Patton explained why the general was no good:

> *I offered him a lesser command in another division, but he told me he needed forty-eight hours to consider it. I did not tell him so, but I realized that any man who could not make up his mind in less than forty-eight hours, was not fit to command troops in battle.*

The same conditions can exist in the business environment. Mangers who need to be aware of *all* the information on a subject before they decide are really not making decisions at all. With *all* the information present, one merely arrives at a logical conclusion, which has no element of risk.

FLEXIBILITY

If there is one statement by Patton that deserves a big frame and a big wall, it's this:

There is no "approved" solution to any tactical situation.

Patton believed in flexibility to meet changing needs. Circumstances certainly alter cases. He relied on his cleverness and creativity and never committed himself to an irrevocable direction or course. Once when planning an assault, Eisenhower's command omitted the proper use of smoke in obscuring the troops from the enemy. Patton pointed out the omission and was stunned by the reply: "Major Murphy told me that he could not add smoke because the stencils for the plan had already been cut." Patton prevailed, but the major in question was willing to endanger an assault rather than take the trouble to have new stencils cut. Such destructive inflexibility can also occur in management, especially when one considers how much money is wasted in companies by employees with similar attitudes.

When employees are not motivated to think independently, they process everything by rote. When they are allowed to forget that procedures are to be used as guidelines, not as commandments, the cost of inflexibility increases and the quality of morale decreases.

Inflexibility contributes to another wasteful condition in business called functional fixedness. This is the tendency of an individual to put a functional value on an object, and once that value is established, the individual can see no other use for the object. A piece of inspection equipment that may have many and diverse uses but is used in only one specific test will lead the technician to assume that it has only one function. When the need for a different test arises, a new piece of equipment will be procured while the first piece lies idle. Functional fixedness impairs flexibility.

The history of American business offers numerous examples of incredibly good managers who made incredibly good and bad decisions. When Henry Ford decided to employ a moving assembly line, when he decided to give his employees a living wage, and when he decided to produce a low cost "black" car, he exhibited good decision making. When he decided that Hitler was merely misunderstood, he made a very poor decision when he sailed to Europe to intercede. If today's managers make nothing but good decisions, they are either making too few of them or running against the odds. A poor decision occasionally should not cause the manager too much concern. Bad decisions, as well as good ones, must, as Patton advised, be kept in perspective.

I have a notion that usually the great things a man does appear to be great only after we have passed them. When they are at hand they are normal decisions and are done without knowledge. In the case of a general, for example, the almost super human knowledge which he is supposed to possess exists only in the mind of his biographer.

SUMMARY

Although the circumstances and exigencies of war and business differ considerably, comparisons can be made. In both cases, decisions must by definition involve some risk. By defining the risk and understanding the correct purpose of the decision, the decision maker has a greater chance of success. Special care should be taken when an unpopular decision must be rendered, and commitment must be forceful.

A deliberate process can be followed to minimize the error probability by (1) using a ladder of abstraction, (2) selecting the correct decision purpose, (3) developing qualities of alternative methods, (4) evaluating each one, and (5) deciding the best alternative to be implemented. Time spent engaged in this process is never wasted, but conditions may not permit the full use of this procedure.

Timing is a critical element of the decision-making process, and decisions can be made too early or too late. Morale problems are caused by one that are made too late.

PATTON SAID:	A GOOD MANAGER:
☐ "You must be simple minded."	☐ Commits himself to his decisions.
☐ "All kinds of people will try to subvert your decisions."	☐ Keeps in mind the potential roadblocks to a decision.
☐ "Don't keep changing your decisions."	☐ Uses expert advice.

PATTON SAID:	A GOOD MANAGER:
☐ "Act like a commander."	☐ Accepts responsibility for decisions.
☐ "Lacking orders is no excuse for inaction."	☐ Ensures that all employees are gainfully employed.
☐ "If a man needs 48 hours to make up his mind, he's not fit to command."	☐ Makes decisions in a timely manner.

)

Chapter 8
CREATIVITY

Genius Is an Immense Capacity for Taking Pains

I find that moral courage is the most valuable and usually the most absent characteristic in men. Much of our trouble is directly attributable to the fear of "they."

The "they" to which Patton referred has terminated the creative suggestions in many management discussions. In fact, "studied opinion" is one of the best inhibitors to creativity that exists. Experts tell us . . .; psychologists tell us . . .; the home office always says . . . : These are some of the culprits in the "they" category that no one ever seems to identify. And anyone who asks, What experts? Which psychologists? Who in the home office? invites looks of disbelief from anyone present as well as the indignant response, "Who are you to question the experts?"

Patton was well known for his creative tactics, his creative language, and his creative role playing. Enemy generals cited creativity as one of his chief assets. It is treated here because of its valuable contribution to successful leadership.

WHAT IS CREATIVITY?

An article in *Forbes* magazine, May 16, 1988, describes the importance of creativity in business. It reprints a speech delivered to training personnel by John Cleese of Monty Python fame, in which Cleese claims that "for a group to function more creatively, people must lose their inhibitions." He also stresses the importance of learning from mistakes and admitting mistakes.

The importance of creativity in a business organization has always been recognized, and creativity is one of the most controversial talents of our day. Psychologists and behavioral scientists worship it, and just about everybody tries to describe it, measure it, and classify it. It remains elusive. Cleese says that the essence of creativity is not in a special talent but in the ability to play with a problem. The brilliant inventor C. F. Kettering thought that "an inventor is a fellow who doesn't know anything about the subject at all and therefore is willing to try something." Creativity has been described as the disposition to make and to organize valuable innovations. Carl B. Rogers calls the creative process the "emergence in action of a novel relational product, growing out of the uniqueness of the individual."[1]

When asked to describe a creative person the average individual will mention an inventor, composer, artist, author, or musician. But when questioned further, the person will readily agree that a housewife is creative, a fireman is creative, and a truck driver is creative. In fact, everybody is creative. It would seem quite apparent that there is no "one" creative process, and there may well be as many creative processes as there are creative people. Obviously, there are many definitions of creativity, but most authorities would agree that creativity is the process of finding new patterns by combining other things.

Creativity expands the possible alternatives to a business decision and the more alternatives developed, the more probability for an especially effective one to emerge. The more creativity exhibited, the more opportunity to take advantage of business situations to expand profit potential.

INHIBITORS TO CREATIVITY

An individual's creative ability can be improved with a conscious effort. The first step is to recognize those things that retard or destroy creative efforts.

Along with studied opinion, the fear of failure also holds a prominent

---

[1]*Kaiser Aluminum News,* Vol. 25, No. 3. "You and Creativity." Kaiser Aluminum & Chemical Corp., Oakland, CA., 1968, p. 3.

place in a list of inhibitors. In the halls of American business, failure is not looked upon kindly. In fact, not trying and therefore not failing is often considered a step above failure. This fear of failure has fostered many inert middle managers who are entirely satisfied with the status quo. They learned early in their business careers that new concepts, although avidly praised and invited, are really not wanted.

To be more successful one has to learn how to fail intelligently. When Thomas Edison was developing the storage battery, he failed at his first eighty or so designs. When asked if he were depressed by his failures, he answered, "No I now know eighty ways of how not to design a battery." Yet Henry Morton, the president of Stevens Institute of Technology, protested against the trumpeting of the results of Edison's experiments in electrical lighting as a "wonderful success" when "everyone acquainted with the subject will recognize it as a conspicuous failure."

In Boston, when Joshua Coppersmith was arrested for trying to sell stock in the recently invented telephone, the court decreed that "all well-informed people know that it is impossible to transmit the human voice over a wire." William James, the noted psychologist and philosopher of the early 1900s observed: "First a new theory is attacked as absurd; then it is admitted to be true, but obvious and insignificant; finally it is seen to be so important that its adversaries claim that they themselves discovered it." James may not have had in mind business management when he made this observation, but the same thing occurs in business.

New ideas are rarely received with enthusiasm. As C. F. Kettering said:

> *Man is so constituted as to see what is wrong with a new thing—not what is right. To verify this, you have but to submit a new idea to a committee. They will obliterate ninety percent of the rightness for the sake of ten percent wrongness. The possibilities a new idea opens up are not visualized because not one man in a thousand has imagination.*

George Patton was a man of imagination. He entertained novel ideas and exploited many situations with less than textbook solutions. Sometimes he would attack over the most difficult terrain and find it the least defended and therefore it could be captured with fewer than average casualties. The enemy could not predict his actions because he was so imaginative. He claimed:

Apparent strength sometimes produces weakness because people are not inclined to occupy strong positions with as many men as they should.

It was this kind of creative thinking that allowed Patton not only to win battles, but to do so without unnecessarily risking the lives of his men.

Pressure to conform is another inhibitor to creativity that has definite application in the world of management. It is like adult peer-group pressure. It is noticeable in dress, in punctuality, in schedule, and in the abundance of "yes men." This is not to say, however, that conformity should be banished and that chaos should be invited to take its place. Conformity is important and necessary in any concerted effort. But in the generation of ideas, conformity adds nothing.

Even in the regimented environment of the military, Patton did not conform. His uniforms were usually different, his pistols were different, and his attitude not quite in sync with those of his contemporaries. He didn't do things differently simply because he didn't want to conform. Each instance of nonconformity had a purpose and a message. At one time he designed a uniform for tankers that consisted of a green jumpsuit with diagonal buttons topped with a football helmet. It didn't catch on and for a while he was referred to as the "Green Hornet." He designed the uniform to instill a certain pride in the tank units. Instead it created some humor.

A Brookings Institute study once concluded that the more education a person had, the less likely he was to be an inventor. Educational constraints inhibit creativity by developing an unquestioning acceptance of already existing things.

General Patton was aware that education could be a detriment to creative approaches if not tempered by experience. In fact, in combat he would occasionally place a new replacement captain under the command of a seasoned lieutenant until a certain amount of experience under fire had been gained by the newcomer.

The fear of new ideas is a formidable barrier to creativity. Patton did not fear new ideas. He created them and welcomed others to offer them. He wanted to hear all of the alternatives prior to making a decision. But once he heard them, he came to a decision quickly. The acceptance of a new idea necessitates innovation of some sort, and the innovation may have an adverse effect on others. The fear of new ideas is closely related to another inhibitor to creativity, contentment with the status quo.

The status quo, to Patton, was anathema. The last thing he ever wanted to do was to stand still. His orders were to attack, attack, and attack and never take a defensive position. During the years between the wars, he was always devising, developing, writing, and changing things, which in a general drove his contemporaries to dislike him. They enjoyed the status quo because of the energy it saved. Creativity required work, but that never bothered Patton.

In 1935 a polo match was being played for the inter-island championship in Hawaii. The Oahu team was captained by Walter Dillingham and Army was captained by Patton, who was a colonel at the time. The match was close and heated, and when Dillingham drove his horse into Patton's, Patton unleashed a string of profanity that carried to the stands and the ears of Gen. Hugh Drum. The general removed Patton as captain of the team, but the opposing team captain, Dillingham, told General Drum that he didn't hear any profanity and that if Patton were not allowed to play the Oahu team would cancel the match immediately. General Drum reinstated Patton, but at the end of Patton's tour of duty in Hawaii he gave Patton the poorest efficiency report in his entire career. It read, in part, that "this officer could be of great value in time of war. He is, however, most disruptive to a command in time of peace." Patton thought it was a great joke and said "the old poop doesn't know it but he's paid me quite a compliment." The General didn't think too much of the status quo.

It is of course far less taxing, far less risky, and far safer politically to do something the same way that it's been done before than to institute a new order of things. As Niccolo Machiavelli expressed in *The Prince:*

> *It must be considered that there is nothing more difficult to carry out, nor more doubtful of success, nor more dangerous to handle than to initiate a new order of things. For the reformer has enemies in all those who profit by the old order, and only lukewarm defenders in all those who would profit by the new order, this lukewarmness arising partly from fear of their adversaries, who have the law in their favor; and partly from the incredulity of mankind, who do not truly believe in something new until they have had the actual experience of it.*

Patton was not afraid of the "new order of things." As his nephew observed: "He was ridiculed and bitterly criticized for having always kept in the forefront of his mind, and so spoken clearly and loud of, that which he believed best for his country. He would, since this was his basic make-up, shock, anger, but also charm many people; and he would hurt himself badly in the eyes of others."

As for peer pressure, Patton did not bend to it and had some strong words on breaking tradition:

> *There was a tradition, or at least a habit, at West Point called the Silence. This was: when one officer whom the cadets felt had behaved poorly toward them came into the mess hall, the corps would rise to attention and remain entirely silent at the meal thereafter. One day when I happened to be in command of the battalion and was bringing them into the hall, I sensed that a "silence" was about to be put on against a young officer. I felt they were wrong about the man and I was opposed in any event to the practice. Therefore, I surprised the hell out of them. I called the battalion to attention and marched them right back to quarters—and without lunch. The young officer called me down for breaking tradition; but I think I convinced him I was right. A man knows instinctively he is right.*

In a lighter vein, creativity was shown by the General in taking a difficult situation and turning it into a benefit. Early in his career he was fox hunting with his daughter when a rider who was totally out of control just missed his daughter's horse and she narrowly escaped certain injury. Patton galloped to the offender and, as described by his daughter, "cursed steadily for three minutes without repeating himself once. It was amazing." The offender was a high-ranking military attaché from Argentina, and Patton was ordered by his commander to prepare and submit a letter of apology to the man. Surprisingly, the attaché replied that "he enjoyed the United States, the great sport of hunting and the fox, and he was complimented that the American major had seen fit to refer to him in Anglo-Saxon sporting terms."

DEFINING GENIUS

A study was conducted of mathematicians and chemists who were rated for creativity by their colleagues. They formed two groups and were given a battery of tests to identify specific differences and only two differences were uncovered. One was that the creative group comprised extremely hard-working people and the second was that the creative group was more asocial than social. The creative group almost always chose answers that were the opposite to the majority. No doubt, Patton would be in the creative group. He would go against tradition when he thought it necessary, and he could work hard.

Patton stated his own definition for creativity when he made the following remark:

Genius is an immense capacity for taking pains.

It's pithy and extremely valuable for most managers to remember. Patton believed that creativity was a product of hard work. In fact, he believed just about everything involved hard work. He recognized that someone's action or advice that may have appeared as a product of divine inspiration was in reality a product of experience. And experience, more often than not, is earned through hard work.

PROBLEM SENSITIVITY

An individual who is especially sensitive to problems and can recognize them sooner than the average person seems to exhibit a high degree of creativity. The more sensitive a person is to a problem, the more apt that person is to create solutions to the problem. This sensitivity, some of which may be inherited according to some studies, can be developed and improved with practice. Viewing different things and listing their deficiencies and methods of correcting the deficiencies can make a person more aware of deficiencies. An ordinary bicycle subjected to problem sensitivity analysis at a seminar revealed the following lack:

☐ Pants catch on chain   ☐ Hard to learn to ride

☐ Tires go flat   ☐ Too large to transport

☐ It falls down   ☐ No weather protection

☐ Hard to pedal   ☐ Difficult to ride in sand and mud

☐ Seat is uncomfortable   ☐ Costs too much

☐ Needs lubrication   ☐ It cannot back up

☐ Difficult to climb hills   ☐ Consumes energy

☐ Gets out of adjustment   ☐ Hard to store

☐ No luggage capacity   ☐ Easy to steal

☐ It rusts   ☐ Not fast enough

This list was developed by a small group of children in the fourth grade during a 15-minute period. Continual practice will increase a person's sensitivity and allow one to better identify areas of potential improvement. This practice, however, may contribute to someone adopting a somewhat skeptical attitude and the urge to correct a mistake or lack.

A few corporate problem sensitivity sessions on the prime product, or a company policy or procedure, may be revealing. If a company can develop a sensitivity to costs and instill a cost-sensitive attitude in its employees, the rewards are great. Cost sensitivity differs from the terms *cost-conscious* or *cost awareness* in that these terms do not imply corrective action. Employees can be well aware of excessive or unnecessary costs without ever questioning the value that these costs represent. Employees who are cost-sensitive will, as a rule, challenge those costs they consider improper. Patton displayed his sensitivity to problems every time he encountered a new situation. His attitude was always one of constructive discontent. When confronted with a new situation, he could quickly perceive the problems at hand, then he would set about trying to solve them.

IMPROVING CREATIVITY

The creative ability can be improved through the deliberate use of mental exercises designed to develop the qualities generally attributed to very creative persons. The following specific aids and techniques can be used.

1. *Write down ideas as they occur.* The statement "Don't worry about that now, I'll remember it tomorrow" has sabotaged many a brilliant future and many would-be inventors have remained as such because of the

statement, "I won't write it down, but I'll remember it in the morning." New ideas should be written down as a way to reflect on them and possibly develop better ideas.

2. *Take notes on observations.* This does not mean that the manager should walk around all day with a note pad noting obscure and trivial observations. It does mean that when a potential problem has been identified, the manager should write down observations on areas, items, or people concerning the potential problem. This can vastly improve problem sensitivity, and the notes can be useful in future problem analyses.

3. *Set deadlines and quotas for creative ability.* By setting quotas and deadlines, the manager ensures that alternatives will be considered, especially if the quotas and deadlines are known to others. They then become a challenge. The manager who practices this approach will react to another's assessment that a situation has but one apparent alternative with the statement, "There's got to be at least ten ways that can be performed." If challenged to name them, the manager can probably develop ten to fifteen methods with perhaps one or two creative alternatives. Developing this habit of setting goals and deadlines is the best and most durable technique for increasing creativity.

4. *Establish a specific time and place for creative thinking.* Some people find that a specific set of conditions can assist the creative process. To some, chaos and disorder is stimulating but to most a quiet surrounding helps. Whatever best fits the manager's needs should be established and used.

AIDS TO CREATIVITY

A multiplicity of ideas seems to offer the most promising road to a creative solution, and the aids to generating ideas are many. The more useful ones are those using team participation. The advantages of group sessions are that a free association of ideas is encouraged and the opportunity to develop the ideas of others is increased. Many books have been written on the subject that treat generating new ideas in detail. The few ideas listed here are those that seem to be the most used in business world.

Brainstorming is the technique most commonly used. It was developed by Alex F. Osborn and uses a classroom setting. It employs a team approach with a team consisting of between five and twelve members, preferably with diverse backgrounds. They should be of the same or similar managerial level to maintain an environment free of supervisory duress. The team should be notified of the session early to allow individuals to develop ideas they can introduce at the session. The rules are basically simple:

☐ Judicial judgment and negative comments are ruled out, and wild ideas are not only welcome but also desired.

☐ Hitchhiking on the ideas of others or combining some of the proposed ideas to form new ones is encouraged.

☐ Large quantities of ideas are sought. The more ideas developed, the more potential solutions to the defined problem are discovered. The average team will feel quite satisfied and even smug if it develops fifteen to twenty alternates. "What's tough about this creative thinking?" team members may ask after the first ten minutes have revealed the fifteen most obvious alternatives. When told that the "best" ideas usually occur between the fiftieth and seventy-fifth alternatives, the group becomes subdued. Developing alternatives is hard work and the productivity of the group declines markedly after forty-five minutes to an hour. Generally, sessions should not exceed one hour.

☐ All of the ideas should be recorded so that they are visible to all to allow for future evaluation.

The group can return for another session to evaluate its work, or it can be evaluated by the manager or individual who is most concerned with the problem. In the evaluation process, each listed idea is subjected to a judicial revenue, not for a negative purpose to find fault with the idea but to add something to an almost workable idea to make it workable.

Synectics is a technique created by William J. Gordon that seeks innovative solutions to a specific problem by using analogy in imaginative ways to make the strange familiar and the familiar strange. It requires group participation, and obvious and rational solutions are discarded in favor of eccentric and outlandish ones. It usually results in a dynamic high-energy session where members use four basic types of analogy:

1. Personal analogy is where the team member tries to identify with the object of the sessions. "How would I feel if I were . . . ?"

2. Symbolic analogy is where the team through an association of metaphors develops images that look at the problem in an inaccurate but imaginative manner. "Imagine a blackboard being erased by a windshield wiper but it can recall messages like a computer terminal."

3. Direct analogy make a real comparison between parallel facts in different applications. "Could we learn how to develop a better carpet by observing how a dog turns around five times before he sits?"

4. Fantasy analogy tries to make a link between the world as it is and a fantasy world. "If a carpet could fly, what kind of urban transportation could we build?"

Synectics requires an experienced session leader and a very willing and dynamic team member.

Morphological analysis and *attribute listing* are techniques that can be effectively used without a team effort. In attribute listing an attribute of one thing can create new ideas by combining it with a known object, resulting in a useful new product: combining the object of a house with the attribute of air conditioning might have given someone the idea for the air-conditioned auto. In morphological analysis the problem area or product is broken down into basic attributes, and a list of alternatives is developed for each attribute on a separate slip. If the product were a "blender," then the attribute slips might appear in this form:

POWER SOURCE	CONTAINER GEOMETRY	CONTAINER MATERIAL	CUTTING METHODS
Electric	Cylinder	Glass	Knife—rotary
Steam	Square box	Steel	Knife—reel
Solar	Triangular	Plastic	Knife—vertical
Gas	Oval	Cloth	Air
Wind	Round	Paper	Flame
Geothermal	Rectangular	Leather	Water

By comparing one attribute with another, moving one slip up and down compared to the others, a great many new ideas are formed. A wind-powered, leather oval container with a high pressure air cutting action may result in a new camping product.

ATTRIBUTES OF A CREATIVE PERSON

Managers who want to inject more creativity in their daily operations can emulate the attributes of a highly creative person by remembering and reviewing these attributes often:

☐ *Problem sensitivity*—Be aware of the existence of the problem

☐ *Idea frequency*—Produce ideas in quantity

☐ *Flexibility*—Be adaptive in the approach

☐ *Originality*—Try for new and unique ideas

☐ *Constructive discontent*—Seek improvement

☐ *Observation*—Be alert to the environment

☐ *Facility at combination*—Combine in variety

☐ *Orientation*—Become disposed toward creativity

☐ *Motivation*—Develop the desire, drive, and energy required to succeed

☐ *Disregard of criticism*—Encourage new ideas

☐ *Vision*—Look for quality

Patton contained the listed attributes in varying degrees and his success in battle was based, at least partially, to his use of the creative approach. Creativity enhances success in just about any endeavor and Patton applied it liberally.

SUMMARY

The restraints to creativity cannot be eliminated by mere commands. They are with us for life. But the manager who is aware of these inhibitors when they are present can consciously combat them. Fear of failure, studied opinion, pressure to conform, and contentment with the status quo are the elements of mediocrity. Managers who don't consider themselves highly creative can exploit techniques and aids to improve their creativity. Patton proved that the creative approach fosters success. The most beneficial action a manager or company can take is to establish a climate of acceptance of new ideas. When new ideas are solicited, considered, and rewarded, then creativity becomes part of the standard operating procedures and everybody wins.

PATTON SAID:	A GOOD MANAGER:
☐ "Much of the trouble is the fear of 'they.'"	☐ Combats inhibitors to creativity.
☐ "Apparent strength produces weakness."	☐ Looks for the novel solution.
☐ "Genius is an immense capacity for taking pains."	☐ Realizes that creativity requires hard work.
☐ "Attack, attack, and then attack."	☐ Isn't satisfied with the status quo.

Chapter 9
PRODUCTIVITY

Make Sure the Troops Get What They Want in Time

Wars may be fought with weapons but they are won by soldiers.

The output is what counts, and experts report that output in American businesses is dwindling. Some blame it on "employee withdrawal" where the dissatisfied workers come to work late, slip out early, and take long lunch periods. Also drugs, alcohol, and stealing from the company, which seem to be on the rise, contribute to the problem. Many solutions to the productivity problem have been proposed by the experts but, each one that is offered seems to create the potential for greater problems. Tying pay to performance, retraining employees out of dull and routine jobs, spotlighting top performers, and firing unproductive employees are some of the solutions offered. Each proposal has merits and also the potential to backfire.

Productivity problems were not high on Patton's daily agenda. He figured that if a leader planned well, motivated, promoted teamwork, created high morale, and made sure people knew what they were supposed to do and why, productivity would result automatically. But Patton did have a few words on other things that affect productivity.

LINE AND STAFF

The subject of the organizational relationship of line and staff has been well covered in textbooks and business periodicals. There are myriad theories on how it facilitates productivity. Patton's theory was very simple:

> *The chief purpose of the General and Special staffs is to ensure that the troops get what they want in time.*

The General and Special staffs can be equated to purchasing, production control, accounting, or any other service department of a company. The "troops" in business are, of course, the people who produce the product. Often, in practical business workings, staff or service organizations forget or overlook their dependence on the line organizations. When they do this, they assume an attitude of independence that can inhibit economical production severely. Staff or service organizations should be reminded frequently of their primary function, which is to serve.

Often when the basic function "to serve" is not well expressed and emphasized, the staff organizations will develop their own "basic function." The personnel department will determine that its basic function is to determine, select, and recruit company employees rather than assisting other departments in their quest for employees. Accounting will determine that it has the divine right to allocate moneys to other departments based on its own judgment and procedures. Quality control will determine that its basic function is "to reject parts" instead of assisting other departments in trying to reduce rejection rates. In fact, the staff organizations will try to function as line organizations, ignoring their true responsibilities.

Staff independence and isolation can also promote a reaction from line management. In this "game-playing" form of management, line managers are not to be denied their "times at bat." The lack of cooperation and action by the staff affords the line organizations a bottomless bag of excuses. "Production is delayed because purchasing (any staff organization can be inserted) hasn't furnished the tools we need." Patton's answer was:

> *The combat service and not the supply service is responsible for failure to get such things.*

Therefore, if line management had appraised the situation and had planned properly, and had instituted controls, the necessary tools would have been provided.

Unless line and staff management function as a "united family," productivity will greatly suffer. A lot of wasteful activity will be generated in interdepartmental rivalry. In this game, some departments may emerge as winners, but there will be one big loser—the company.

PROPER TOOLS FOR THE JOB

To initiate production without the items necessary to accomplish it is tantamount to preparing for failure. Yet, it happens everyday in management—usually on a high level: "I want thirty units out the door by the end of the month," orders the vice president of operations who has just been exposed to the president's wrath in a staff meeting.

"But we don't have the parts, the materials, the tools, and the engineering drawings," pleads the director of manufacturing.

"I don't care, just do it," yells the vice president.

Then the fun begins. The orderly and efficient production system comes to a halt. Purchasing scurries around to find parts for immediate delivery and when available pays a 100 percent premium. Production employees begin ten-hour days, seven days a week, and the fatigue factors—to say nothing of morale—cause a rejection rate that would make the most hardened quality control manager sob.

Engineering documentation bypasses the checking procedure and is issued to the production department with the designer still adding dimensions in transit. Final testing is averted, for, since no one knows how it's supposed to work, testing becomes academic. Quality control, with closed eyes, stamps the finished products, and on the thirtieth of the month ten units, not thirty, are shipped.

On the fifteenth of the following month ten units are received back for repair or replacement.

All this is caused by initiating a production plan without providing the required tools.

The General provided those who carried out his plans the best tools possible. He wanted the best cooks for his men; he spent time assuring that his troops had good and sufficient food and clothing; he believed ammunition should be expended not hoarded; and when his subordinates didn't know how to accomplish the plan, he was always present for consultation.

Patton also believed that his superiors should provide him with the means to do his job and, on occasion, quietly suggested this to them. When his armies reached the German front, he thought that with fresh logistical support he could reach Berlin in two weeks. He sent a wire to the commanding general, ComZone, in Paris: "Have just pissed in the Rhine. For God's sake send gasoline."

OVERHEAD

George Patton believed in "producing" organizations and when riflemen were needed he ordered a five or ten percent cut in management of army and corp overhead to get the needed riflemen. He chided Eisenhower for not doing the same in higher echelons. He figured he could have ended the war six months earlier had Ike followed his example. Also, he described an overhead phenomenon that is seen occasionally in business and really adds to the overhead expense. It's called "assistants to":

> *The assistants that collect around a staff officer in a few months is awful and unnecessary. This fungus growth is caused by the natural middle-agedness of the man and by the foolish desire of young officers to become the nth assistant something or other.*

In the growth of a young company, "assistant to" labels are rarely seen because the company must stay trim to maintain its fighting weight. But when the company matures, an "assistant to" pops up in every department, and the managers wonder why profits begin to dwindle. If the overhead was unnecessary in the growth stage, there's a good chance that it is also unnecessary in the nature stage—unless an overweight condition is desired.

Many large companies have succumbed to the practice of rewarding excellence in line management with promotions to staff management and the pattern followed during the company's life cycle is interesting and almost amusing to observe. A company assumes geometric shapes of a triangle, square and an inverse triangle. Each shape has its own impact on profitability and the nature of the extent of change indicates an almost

Figure 1.

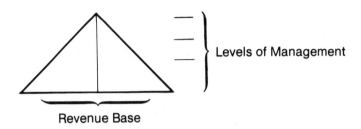

natural involvement. It could be termed the theory of the inverse triangle. The normal geometric figure that a small company assumes is the isosceles triangle (see Figure 1). The president leads the company and as it grows, each subordinate level expands. The revenue-producing level is at the base of the triangle. Therefore the larger the base, the larger the income. This shape seems to be conducive to profits and exists because of the need to survive. When money is tight and survival uncertain, the height of the triangle must be minimized, because each level above the base produces less and less income.

As money becomes more plentiful, and as success is tasted, expansion is inevitable. More divisions are formed and the triangle slowly evolves into the square with the addition of many staff people (see Figure 2).

Figure 2.

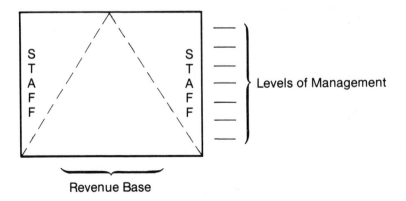

Figure 3.

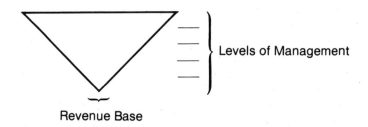

Revenue Base

These people are usually cronies of the president who have served him well in line functions and are rewarded by promotion to staff. The procedure normally followed is: (1) announcement of the promotion, and (2) determination of the job function of the new position. (The newly promoted executive usually prepares the description of the new function, which is typically a duplication of something done at a lower level.) In the new corporate configuration, the revenue base remains proportional to the previous shape.

The executives cannot operate without staff, so each hires at least three directors. The directors in turn, each hire three managers to keep the organization chart symmetrical, and so on, down to the level that does the work.

Since the revenue base of the square configuration has remained proportionally stable, while the cost of operations has nearly doubled, the company's ability to compete is jeopardized. The evolution from the square to the inverse triangle begins. The time phase for the complete change varies with general economic conditions. A declining economy hastens the change appreciably. The change involves terminating people, but surprisingly there is no attempt to revert to the triangular model. Since the large corporate staff is comprised of friends of the president and since he established the staff originally, the cutback of personnel must begin at the bottom. An arbitrary percentage of employees in those organizations below the staff level are terminated. This is done of course by the corporate staff, which eliminates any need for personal involvement by the president. All distasteful decisions and emotional conflicts are anticipated and prevented. As the revenue base is reduced, the situation becomes more acute until the inverse triangle is completed (see Figure 3). At this point bankruptcy is imminent. Patton probably would label this type of company as an excellent example of "fungus growth."

STRATEGY AND TACTICS

Productivity at all levels of management can be enhanced by the use of strategy and tactics, and the higher the level the more return.

The bookshelves of business libraries are not crammed with volumes on business strategy and tactics. The terms have had almost exclusive use in the military. Strategy—defined as the science of planning and directing operations—can be compared to the management functions. Tactics—the science of maneuvering military forces—may be compared to the use of clever means to attain the objectives of the management functions.

Cleverness or tactics in management is often thought to be a spontaneous move of a creative individual and when first employed probably was. When the clever act was repeated in subsequent similar conditions, it became a tactic. These tactics cover a spectrum of uses and are difficult to classify. They can involve flexibility, boldness, decision making, knowledge of the competition, treatment of employees, proper timing, and other topics, and they are seldom made public. They usually are jealously guarded, characteristic traits and if they are revealed they appear as the all-knowing type of motto that adorn many office walls.

The manager should be aware that tactics and strategy can effect productivity. He should try to develop his own by specifying a specific strategy after defining each goal or objective. If the goal is to ship 150 units per month and the plant capacity is taxed at 100 units per month, the strategy of using the company's resources to accomplish the goal should be defined. The tactics show up later in the clever means taken to offset problems:

> *Good tactics can sometimes save even the worst strategy, but bad tactics can ruin even the best strategy.*

Patton liked to use steamroller strategy but not steamroller tactics:

> *. . . that is, make up your mind on course and direction of action and stick to it. But in tactics, do not steamroller. Attack weakness. Hold them by the nose and kick them in the ass.*

For Patton, the simplest and best strategy was one that could, with mild adjustment, be applied to business operations:

Find out what the enemy intend to do and do it first.

This may have some application in the marketing and product planning area in a highly competitive industry where market dominance is very important. Constant evaluation of industry data, intelligence input from trade shows, salesmen's rumors, and vendor comments can allow a company to forecast a competitor's plans for the future. This knowledge of probable course can open many avenues of action. In business as in war, forewarned is forearmed.

If a company is the leader in an industry and wishes to remain so, the company's product planning organization might well adopt another of Patton's suggestions:

> *Rock the enemy back on their heels. Keep him rocking back and never give him a chance to get his balance or to build up.*

Competitive advantage is often the key to business survival and long-range, or for that matter, short-range planners might do well to consider some of Patton's observations regarding terrain features:

> *Always capture the highest terrain features in your vicinity at once, and stay on it.*

Corporate planners should survey the spectrum of business positions or "business terrain features" and select those that promise the best competitive position. Then, capture those positions rapidly and stay in the lead. These features may be prospective clients, geographical areas, or other elements that contribute to a competitive lead. One sale to General Motors or Boeing or Shell Oil may be far more important than a sale of thousands to small unknown firms in terms of future competitive position. If a presence in a certain geographical area is important competitively, it should be identified and accommodated in the company plan. New product introduction can be extremely susceptible to "taking the high ground." If you don't, someone else will. Complacency in a lead position has hastened the demise of many companies.

TRAINING

Any thorough discussion on productivity has got to include the topic of employee training. To Patton, training consisted of discipline, a knowledge of history, and practicing offensive tactics. Defensive tactics never posed a problem to his army. His orders were that troops, once billeted, rested, and equipped be given constant practice in offensive tactics. And he recognized the propensity for unnecessary training. In Letter of Instruction No. 2 he wrote:

> *There is a tendency for the chain of command to overload junior officers with excessive training requirements. You will alleviate this burden of eliminating nonessential demands.*

Many companies offer training programs with a smorgasbord flavor that are comprised of a variety of training classes devoid of organization, without coherence, and completely divorced from need. As the smorgasbord meal, the training table is piled high with course selections and there is no designated beginning or end. The nutritional value of both is questionable.

Often, the training programs are voluntary and are conducted outside of the normal working hours and the employees that really need the training, such as the low achievers, never attend. The ones who do attend probably don't need it. Management training should accommodate defined needs and defined employees.

Management education is necessary and few in management will disagree. They will affirm the reasons and needs in their budget justification. Management education:

☐ Allows managers to perform current jobs capably and to work for optimum productivity.

☐ Allows managers to gain competency in new technical areas to hold or gain competitive advantage.

☐ Allow managers to manage change effectively in a fast-changing business environment.

☐ Increases the value of the company's investment in its managers.

These reasons are so evident, but there remains one large problem: Management simply does not believe in management education. Not too many managers would voice their agreement with that, but they know in their hearts that the statement is fact. A brief review of management practices attests to a definite lack of belief.

1. *The training budget* created by the manager at budget time is used by many as a contingency account for future budget cutbacks or overruns in other accounts. This hardly indicates management's strong belief in management education.

2. *The attitude* that is shown in the typical manager's appraisal of a fellow management education plan is generally negative. The attitude can be caused by a fear of new ideas, the sense that "managers are born not made," the perception that "a manager is a manager is a manager," charlatans selling management education, and the lack of immediate and measurable results.

3. *The abstract statements* used to describe educational needs signal managerial indifference. To improve managerial effectiveness, to improve interpersonal communications, to stay abreast of the state-of-the-art advances, and to develop managerial skills are some of the key phrases that imply only cursory interest in, and knowledge of, management education. Often, the management education program does not reflect realistic educational needs and if any are satisfied they are done so by sheer chance.

Management seems to be continually seeking some form of management education that will provide a cure for all management ills. That one easily understood, easily applied, and always effective management technique that will relieve the manager of the bothersome problems of decision making is not only eagerly sought after but, worse, is promised by many training specialists. When the utopian education program is found lacking, the manager's doubts in management education are strengthened.

The problem that managers do not believe in management education must be solved by, of all things, education of management. To do this, the types of management education currently available, and methods of providing it, should be identified and then examined in terms of existing and future needs. From this analysis, a positive management education image can evolve.

The types of management education that are most prominent are four: (1) management oriented, (2) people oriented, (3) function oriented, and (4) technical oriented.

☐ *Management-oriented courses*—those that supply the fundamentals of total management, including philosophy. These courses are usually directed at the neophyte manager and are looked upon by those in upper management as a primer course unworthy of their attention. This is unfortunate because the principles of managing are not unlike the principles of any philosophy. They must be reinforced periodically so they become the underlying foundation for all management action. Company management would do well to develop a refresher course for all managers. Patton ensured that all of his officers could operate their assigned weapon by periodic testing. The lament that "I did it once before" would not satisfy the periodic requirement. Just because managers took management courses years ago is no assurance that they are using the principles now.

☐ *People-oriented courses*—those that are allied to the behavioral approaches of management are difficult to assess. Their popularity is waning and they should be able to survive strict scrutiny before they are selected. The results must be measurable.

☐ *Function-oriented courses*—those directed toward a particular function or discipline of management, for example, "planning," should satisfy a specific need for a specific person or group of people.

☐ *Technical-oriented courses*—those that answer the "how" rather than the "what" or "why" are becoming more and more important and more and more numerous. There are thousands of courses being offered in some phase of computer technology and the advertisements that are mailed to business state that this particular one is a necessity for every manager in business. "The Impact that Artificial Intelligence will have on Future Management Decisions," for example, may be a fun course to attend, discuss, and debate, but its need is far from pertinent in today's market. Artificial intelligence is in its infancy and years from full implementation. Again, return on investment in a reasonable time period should be the selection criterion.

The vehicles to provide management education are: (1) company developed and conducted training programs, (2) public seminars, (3) internal seminars by consultants, and (4) university programs. Each has advantages and problems.

☐ Company developed and conducted programs—often used effectively in basic-skills training for factory workers, many times lacks the image necessary for effective management education training and tend to suffer from a lack of direction.

☐ *The public seminar*—a favorite of many employees especially when the seminar is conducted in the Sun Belt during the winter. There can be problems where the seminar is more often an employee fringe benefit rather than serious management education, but often the training is not offered otherwise. There is one benefit that is not available in the other methods, and that is the information to be gained from other company employees attending the same seminar. Often a camaraderie develops among the attendees, which in turn provides an honest appraisal of the industry and a rapport that lasts long after the seminar.

☐ *Internal seminars*—conducted on company premises by a training organization or consultant and offer a good deal more benefit than do public seminars. At least on the surface they do. The employees are acquainted with company operations; the training examples can be relevant; the training schedule can be the normal work schedule; and the cost is usually lower. The problem with conducting internal seminars is that many managers will send only those employees who "can be spared," which means those approaching retirement, marginal performers, and employees who are between assignments.

☐ *University programs*—with many continuing courses of education for business that can offer a wide array of management courses. They are specifically designed to keep the busy manager appraised of new business techniques. The cost is usually significant, and they can contain the same pitfalls as public seminars. Also, there is a likelihood of the program being too academic to meet the needs of the trainee.

How would Patton have handled management education as a company CEO? Probably he would have a vice president of training whose purpose it would be to ensure that training be related to assisting employees to know what they were supposed to do and why, and probably he would have used Kipling's six honest serving men, why? what? when? how? where? and who? prior to approving the budget allocation. Most certainly his management would really believe in management education.

SUMMARY

Patton assumed that productivity would occur naturally if leadership, planning, and high morale were present. He had definite thoughts regarding the elements of productivity. He knew that the combat soldier was the essence of army productivity and established a class understanding of line and staff relationships. The staff exists to ensure the troops get what they want in time, but the ultimate responsibility for getting their things rests in the combat troops themselves.

Patton believed that to be productive, people had to have the tools to do the tasks that they are directed to do. Managers must ensure that their employees are provided tools to do the job accordingly.

Although not a problem in army circles, overhead is a potential problem in business. Patton stated that "assistants to" are awful and unnecessary and he would eliminate them to cut his overhead and to increase the ranks of the producing organizations.

He stated that strategy, tactics, and knowing the enemy are important additions to produceability, and that training was an integral function of command. He did not believe in training for the sake of training and directed that unnecessary training be eliminated and that training be focused on the job to be done. Management could learn from his attitude and develop and provide meaningful management education programs. Companies have got to commit themselves to management education rather than treating it as "something nice to do if we had the money." It is not an option in management.

A realistic management education program must be developed that will permit the manager to do his current job more productively, to gain competence in new areas, and to react quickly to changing business climates. The methods of training should be compared and the best combination of methods selected. Each management education program should consist of only those elements that increase the manager's value to the company and yield a higher return on investment.

PATTON SAID:	A GOOD MANAGER:
☐ "Staff functions to serve."	☐ Defines staff responsibilities clearly and reminds staff of them often.
☐ "The combat troops are responsible."	☐ Holds line organizations responsible for what they do.
☐ "'Assistants to' are a fungus growth."	☐ Views "assistants to" with a critical eye.
☐ "Bad tactics can ruin the best strategy."	☐ Relates to the importance of carrying out the job correctly.

PATTON SAID: A GOOD MANAGER:

☐ "Find out what the enemy in-   ☐ Keeps apprised of competi-
tends to do."   tive plans.

☐ "Eliminate nonessential train-   ☐ Develops a training program
ing requirements."   to fit the needs.

Chapter 10
ORGANIZATION

The Proper Time and the Proper Place

To achieve harmony in battle, each weapon must support the other. Team play wins. You "musicians" of Mars must not wait for the band leader to signal to you. You must, each of your volition, see to it that you come into this concert at the proper time and at the proper place.

Organization has been defined as the gathering of all necessary resources at the proper time, in the proper quantity to assure fulfillment of a plan. But for some companies, organization is the placement of square or rectangular images joined by horizontal and vertical lines on a piece of paper. Dotted lines may be used, but lines on the bias or curved lines are forbidden. It seems that the most important thing is the balance; the arrangement of the figures must be balanced to the top block. Then each block is defined and individual names and titles are inserted. Where it is difficult to define the function, the word *coordination* is often used. Patton long ago realized the ambiguous usage of the word: "It is my opinion that coordination is a much misused word and its accomplishment is difficult."

The concept of organization in many companies is totally encompassed in charts depicting job titles and employee names. Is there organization? Just look at all the charts. In theory, organization goes somewhat deeper. Getting it all together takes both "an organization" and "organization." An organization is two or more persons acting in concert to accomplish a common goal. Organization, on the other hand, is the management function that is performed by an organization to pull together all the resources needed in the right place at the right time. It's people getting to the concert at the proper time and at the proper place.

NEW ORGANIZATIONS

Creating a new organization usually has inhibiting factors that control growth. Since most companies start small, the organizers have their grandiose ideas limited by the amount of cash, credit, and credit cards they have. They realize that the product is the thing, and they can wait for their plush offices, complete with private baths and beverage bars until success has been achieved. Growth proceeds carefully and frugally, and they try to get the best people they can to produce the best product in a timely fashion. Their overhead is necessarily low.

Those companies that are started with the help of venture capital have their organizations charts prepared for them or dictated by them. Before they will part with dollars, venture capitalists want to see the proposed organization chart with the top three levels of organization defined and identified. The last thing the company founders are thinking is, "Who's going to be our manager of customer service?" They can't project what is going to happen next week with any degree of reliability yet; they have to prepare an in-depth business plan for the venture capitalists for the next five years. The advent of "spread sheet" software programs has increased the detail required, and today even the depreciation expense, by month, is projected in year five, although the company's guesses are based solely on the need to satisfy the venture capitalists requirements. In either case, the limiting factors of too little cash or the meddling of venture capitalists, inhibit excessive growth. The venture capitalists are guarding their investments and rightly so, but sometimes their budgeting procedures fail to recognize the nonlinearity of opportunity because of their lack of thorough knowledge in that specific business. If an opportune moment occurs, a company can't afford to hoard money. Patton at one time had an allowance of 9,000 shells a day. He said:

You either use it or you don't. I would lose more men by shooting 9,000 rounds a day for three days than I would by shooting 20,000 rounds in one day, and probably would not get as far.

Thus, the company founders are restrained from excessive growth by either limited cash or venture capitalist's demands.

EXISTING ORGANIZATIONS

The process from a lean fighting organization to a slightly heavier, and slightly slower organization is generally a gradual one. But invariably, some fat is added. The reasons for this are probably as myriad as the causes of middle-age spread. It can be lack of enthusiastic leadership as the leaders grow older, or it can be an attitude of complacency that they project. Whatever the reasons, the health of the organization should be reviewed on a periodic basis. How do you put a company on a scale to assess its overweight condition? You take an audit.

SPAN OF CONTROL

In organization review, one of the first elements considered is the existing span of control.

How many people should report to a supervisor of an assembly operation? Twenty. How many staff members should a president have? Six. A director should have between three and five managers reporting to him or her and a manager, three to five supervisors. The chairman of the board of directors should have seven directors. Where do these figures originate?

Many large companies define span of control as the number of people reporting to a given job position; each level of management is assigned a specific standard. I imagine that the standards are based on what someone once believed would produce average results with average people. Perhaps these standards are beneficial. They do give the organization chart a balanced pyramid appearance, which is aesthetically pleasing to the structured mind. Why is it then, that reality seldom seems to agree with the standards? Some managers can handle a staff of dozens easily and effectively. They are as completely serene with a huge staff as Arthur Fiedler was with the Boston Pops. Of course each employee has got to know his or her job intimately to permit such smooth functioning, but that is the job of the manager who, like the conductor of an orchestra, is responsible for the training of employees. Some managers are totally confused with a staff of four and require a few "assistants to" to assist them in their management functions. They hold meetings incessantly and augment the meetings with a flow of memos.

ORGANIZATIONAL VALUE

Even if the correct span of control is achieved to everyone's satisfaction and to all published standards, how does a manager assess the state of health of the organization? In essence, how does the manager establish the value of the organization?

An overview is needed to provide perspective. Patton had his war room, which gave him an overall picture of where all his resources were at any one time. Likewise, managers need systems.

One method (established by W. J. Ridge & Associates) is the Productivity Value Systems (PVS). This process provides a new perspective for productivity in business. For example, in a study of a typical engineering department, rather than viewing labor costs as part of the cost category "engineering," PVS breaks down that cost so that it is related to the cost of specific activities within the engineering category, such as dollars spent on design, coordinating, preparing reports, and getting drawings (see Tables 1 and 2). This view of costs can be surprisingly enlightening and provides insight to new management direction.

Productivity Value Systems offers a data base that shows relationships in different perspectives. For example, it will show the cost of "design product" as a percentage of the engineering department labor cost, as a percentage of the total company labor cost, as a relationship to the cost of building the product, and as a relationship to other significant activities in the company and in the engineering department. A company executive whose accounting reports indicated his research and development costs as 10 percent of sales, may perhaps, be intrigued that the cost of "design products" is less, and 1 percent of sales. The executive may want to investigate the other 9 percent.

The PVS output permits the company or any executive who applies these techniques to assess the value obtained from the labor costs expended. If the organization is a manufacturing company, the PVS output may show that the company activities of "design product," "build product," and "sell product" consume only a total of 25 percent of the company's labor cost. This investment perspective will reveal that of each labor dollar spent, only twenty-five cents is being invested in what the company is really trying to do.

By being aware of the relationship presented by PVS, the executive has a practical basis for budgeting and planning, as well as a solid foundation for planning change and cost reallocation.

Above all, PVS separates the concepts of efficiency and value so that a common business error of increasing the efficiency of something that has little or no value can be averted.

In a war zone, George Patton understood the need for achieving this type of perspective. He indicated this when he deduced the number of Germans left by using the total available and then deducting known data to arrive at his estimates. The mental process that Patton exhibited is closely allied to the style of perspective used in PVS.

PVS evolved from a true value engineering outgrowth Value Analysis of Management Practices (VAMP). The original applications of VAMP to organizations entailed substantial time involvement by all of the people in the organization being studied and although the time consumed was rewarded heavily in results attained, a better way of applying these techniques was formulated.

The manager on any level can initiate the process of self-examination. If the engineering manager wants to evaluate his department he would start by defining the departments prime objective, which may be "design products." He would then list all of the activities that his department performs in direct support of attaining the primary objective such as, design parts, design systems, debug systems, document design and prepare manual.

At this point, the director of the survey would determine the level of detail desired for cost data collection. The purpose of collecting data is to determine that portion of total department cost that is used to perform the activities listed and to list those activities beyond those that directly support the departments prime objective and what they cost. If there is sufficient time each employee can be questioned and asked to describe the type of tasks he performs and the amount of time consumed by each. Employees inputs are combined and atypical cost model for the department is constructed on a master chart as in Table 1. This accounts for the total labor costs.

Table 1: Department Cost Model

	HRS/WK (TYPE)
Design parts	260
Integrate systems	60
Debug systems	30
Document design	245
Prepare manuals	135
Assist customers	15
Prepare progress reports	100
Prepare other reports	48
Coordinate with marketing	202
Administration	210
TOTAL WEEKLY HOURS	1,355

At the same time, if each of the major departments in the company were also participating the engineering manager could see how his department integrated with the other departments on a cost/function relationship. But what is more important he can analyze a presentation that highlights apparent ambiguities when the data is compared to business norms as in Table 2.

Many times a company executive will admit readily that the prime purpose of his company is to design, manufacture, and sell a product. One would assume that the cost of running that company would be involved, to a large extent, with the stated functions. When a presentation reveals that these prime functions account for less than 25 percent of total cost, the remaining 75 percent of total cost would be viewed as suspect and perhaps prompt a closer examination of value.

A survey of the engineering department might result in the analysis shown in Table 2.

Table 2: ANALYSIS—Engineering Department

OBJECTIVE:

DESIGN PRODUCT (11 percent of total Company labor cost)
(53 percent of total Engineering department labor cost)

PRIMARY TASKS	PERCENTAGE OF TOTAL DEPARTMENT	PERCENTAGE OF TASK AS PART OF OBJECTIVE	PERCENTAGE OF COMPANY
Design parts	19%	36%	4 %
Integrate system	4	8	.8
Debug system	2	4	.4
Document design	18	33	4
Prepare manuals	10	19	2
TOTALS	53%	100%	11.2%

RELATIONSHIP HIGHLIGHTS

A. Primary task of department only 53 percent of total.
B. Design, integrate, and debug only 25 percent of total activity.
C. Documentation costs almost as much as design.
D. Manuals costs 50 percent of design costs.
E. Design is only 4 percent of total company cost.

The Manager may want to analyze each relationship highlight. In Highlight A, the 53 percent means that of each dollar spent only 53 cents contributed to the department's main objective. After a review the manager may determine that the allocation is within accepted practices for that type of organization in that type of industry. Highlight B can be revealing in that the "doing and creative" tasks are only 25 percent of total cost. Highlights C and D may cause the manager to review their costs with the intent of devising some method that accomplished the basic intent at less cost. Highlight E may or may not initiate a visit to the president's office with a budget adjustment request.

The survey of the manufacturing department might result in the analysis shown in Table 3.

Table 3: ANALYSIS—Manufacturing Department

OBJECTIVE:

MANUFACTURE PRODUCT (19 percent of total company labor cost)
(45 percent of total manufacturing department labor cost)

TASKS	PERCENTAGE OF TOTAL DEPARTMENT	PERCENTAGE OF TASK AS PART OF OBJECTIVE	PERCENTAGE OF COMPANY
Build System	14%	30%	6%
Test System	9	19	3
Buy Parts	7	16	3
Move Parts	5	11	2
Store Parts	2	5	1
Inspect Parts	6	14	3
Ship Product	2	5	1
TOTALS	45%	100%	19%

RELATIONSHIP HIGHLIGHTS

A. Primary task only 45 percent of total department.
B. Building product only 14 percent of department and only 30 percent of activity.
C. Testing costs 64 percent of what building costs.
D. Inspecting costs 32 percent of what building costs.
E. Handling parts costs more than building product.
F. Buying parts costs as much as moving and storing parts.

Even if the study were restricted to these departmental only the costs of the study would be incidental to the benefits gained. The managers would know what is supposed to do compared to what is being done and why. The study results also provide a basis for improvement planning.

It is recognized that the data collection phase is not yet an exact science and must be directed with some judgment and common sense. Accounting methods may be too stringent and time consuming and approximations should be used liberally but judiciously. It is well to remember that the purpose is to highlight significant anomalies in organization and not conduct a time and motion study on each employee. Also it surveys labor costs only but other costs are usually displayed quite adequately in accounting reports. The trend toward service-type companies increases the impact of labor costs.

Of course the optimum advantage of the PVS is when it results in a company-wide presentation that portrays exactly what each organization is contributing to accomplish company aims. Patton would most likely have a completed chart on display at all times in his office. It certainly shows who is supposed to do what.

On a company-wide basis, the PVS chart gives an integrated picture of the company as in Chart 1.

Chart 1: Company PVS Chart

OBJECTIVES:

DESIGN, MANUFACTURE AND SELL PRODUCT

	ENG	MFG	MKT	FIN	PERS
Design	XXXXX XXXXX				
Manufacture		XXXXX XXXXX			
Sell			XXXXX XXXXX XXXXX	XXXXX	
Satisfy customer	XXXXX XXXXX				
Reporting	XXXXX	XXXXX	XXXXX	XXXXX XXXXX	XXXXX XXXXX
Hiring					XXXXX
Employee relations				XXXXX	XXXXX
Coordination	XXXXX XXXXX	XXXXX XXXXX	XXXXX XXXXX	XXXXX XXXXX	XXXXX XXXXX
Maintain records				XXXXX	XXXXX
Administration	XXXXX	XXXXX	XXXXX	XXXXX	XXXXX
Cost reduction		XXXXX			
Maintain facility		XXXXX			
Other	XXXXX	XXXXX	XXXXX	XXXXX	XXXXX
TOTAL HOURS	XXXXX	XXXXX	XXXXX	XXXXX	XXXXX

With this chart, listing all of the major tasks being performed, the time expended for each and the organization doing them, provides the

CEO an interesting and multifaceted management tool. It is an investment tool that displays the labor spent directly supporting the prime objectives of the company. It aids management teamwork in the formation
of the chart and each manager has a clear view of his part in the whole.
It provides a management resources inventory and most importantly fosters functional thinking on the part of management.

By appraising the departmental inputs in relation to the company out-
puts, the CEO should have a better insight into the effects of request for
larger budgets and increased staffing. With this device, across-the-board
reductions need never occur. If business conditions demand a reduction
in staff, the CEO can select for reduction those areas that contribute
marginal value thereby attaining a reduction in costs without a commensurate reduction in the value that those costs represented.

Patton had his "war room" which gave him the overall picture of
where all of his resources were at any one time. The PVC Chart could
provide the CEO at least a modest identification of his personnel resources.

TIMING

In his drive to Bastogne, Patton provided a practical example of complex organization par excellence. Surely he would scoff at some of our
present-day efforts in organizing to complete a task.

It now takes seven years to get final government approval for a proposed nuclear plant. It can take up to two years for a developer to get
local approval to erect a building. It takes a typical committee at least six
months to do anything. Why? Could it be that the planning is somewhat
muddled and therefore organization is hampered? In the Bastogne incident, Patton had foreseen the envelopment of the First Army, and at the
time he mentioned his plan to Ike, he and his staff had already spent four
days and nights planning his attack to free them.

It could be that in the past, the urgency to organize was not as pressing. The function of organization has taken on new importance with the
change in the basic characteristics of business. Industrial robots are ten
times more common in Japanese industries than in American industry.
New product introductions that ten years ago could be planned for a period of three years now must be done in six months or less to remain
competitive. When IBM introduces a new model of their personal computer, clones are in the marketplace within three to six months. A quick

reacting organization is now necessary not only for improved operations but for survival itself.

The rapidity of, and demands for, improvements plus the cries for increased productivity have forced the successful managers to organize quickly and well—probably not to the extent and completeness that Patton displayed, but at least in a more proficient manner than years ago. To do this, the manager must:

☐ Know the resources available.

☐ Know the degree to which these resources are presently committed.

☐ Know the point at which they can be recommitted.

☐ Know the benefit/loss ratio of recommittal.

SUMMARY

Organizational health is difficult to measure, but new organizations have built-in limiters, such as cash and external direction from venture capitalists. The existing organization needs some measuring device and a review of the span of control is not the only measuring device. Productivity Value Systems gives the manager and CEO the ability to view the entire organization in relation to what each unit is supposed to be doing in fulfilling the organization's objectives. The process itself has many advantages and enforces management discipline by directing the manager's attention toward organizational objectives. In collecting the basic data, the manager usually will talk with each employee in a manner that addresses the job the employee is doing. This aids in team building and gives the employee a chance to express his ideas about the job. The method provides a basis for self-improvement by letting the manager determine the relative value of each task output and identifying top-value areas for potential improvement.

On a companywide basis, the method furnishes the CEO with some of the data that Patton was afforded in his war room upon which he based many operational decisions.

Besides the health of an organization, the organization also must be able to react to change in a much more responsive manner than it needed to in the past.

Organization is not only gathering what is needed but also recognizing what is needed. Patton may not have been clairvoyant, but he worked hard and studied well. He used his staff effectively, especially his intelligence units, and adhered to their advice. He knew the functions and composition of all his organizations and never confused their functions. He made the systems he had work. We in business might emulate his success in organization by concentrating on the basics of organization rather than the techniques of organization.

PATTON SAID:	A GOOD MANAGER:
☐ "Know the deployment of your troops."	☐ Has a handle on what his employees are doing and why.
☐ "Come to the concert at the proper time and place."	☐ Develops a quick-reacting organization.

Chapter 11
COMMUNICATION

Keep the Troops Informed

Formal orders will be preceded by letters of instructions and by personal conferences. In this way the whole purpose of the operation will be made clear, together with the mission to be accomplished by each major unit. In this way, if communication breaks down during combat, each commander can and must so act as to attain the general objective.

As the warden in the film *Cool Hand Luke* said to Paul Newman, "What we have here is a failure to communicate," this failure to communicate has been assigned as the efficient cause of just about all business and non-business problems. Management consultants would be at a loss without this convenient scapegoat. Marriage counselors would have to close up shop. Adam and Eve probably had a problem or two due to lack of communication. But "communications" as a problem source is just too abstract a concept to treat. It cannot be measured in cubic yards or square feet and the metric system doesn't help at all. It must be presented in a more concrete form before alternate methods of problem solution can be developed.

If "improving communication" were the subject of a problem solving session, the different methods of communication would be listed as alternative solutions. Semaphore flags, signing, smoke signals, telephone, and telegraph are all methods of communications but hardly solutions to "improving communication." A more concrete definition is required. The alleged communication problem is developed because the problem identified as a communications problem doesn't really know what the problem is or else doesn't want anyone else to know about it. No one ever accused General Patton of having or even being part of a communication problem. Patton simply made sure what he wanted was understood by those from which he desired specific action. Imagine that Patton's teachings in formal orders were applied to business and that all business directives would have been necessarily preceded by letters of instruction and personal conferences. A good portion would never have been issued because the situation requiring the directive would have probably been accommodated in the conferences. Patton realized the potential for misunderstanding in the transmission of ideas and had much to say in the matter.

TELL THE LINEMEN THE PLAY

No one likes to be left in the dark. Patton thought this was an extremely foolish way for an officer to command his troops:

> *Keep the troops informed. Use every measure before and after combat to tell the troops what they are going to do and what they have done.*

People want to know what is going on. Then they can cope with any eventuality. Personnel directors, public relation experts, psychologists, and every manager should heed this advice. The effectiveness of any of the morale-building methods will be directly proportional to the use of this technique. Teamwork is stressed in many management journals and pep talks to employees. But teamwork requires that each member of the team be informed of conditions, plans, and potential outcomes. Consider a football team whose quarterback, when calling plays, excludes the linemen from each huddle: "I'll just tell my close associates, my backfield, what play we're going to run and you linemen just go do whatever it is that you do." In professional football it would be preposterous. In professional management it occurs. For good morale, the troops must be kept informed.

Some experts contend that the cause of many morale problems stems from the nonalignment of the employees' personal goals with the goals of the job and the company. If this is fact, then company managers must start to tell their employees what's going on because withholding information is definitely not in alignment with employees' personal goals.

It is relatively easy to keep people informed. Published departmental plans and objectives, weekly communication meetings, information memos, and personal communications are all low-cost communication media. Seldom are more sophisticated communication techniques required.

COMMUNICATING GOALS AND OBJECTIVES

"How do I get my plans down to all the employees?" asks the harried manager. The answer is, "You don't. Not unless you don't believe in organization. Your job is to communicate your plans to your staff, and they communicate to their staffs, and so on. If they fail, get a new staff." General Patton believed in the simple approach:

> *The best way to issue orders is by word of mouth. . . . Failing this, telephone conversation which should be recorded at each end . . .*

Patton also noted, "My language was not particularly political." It was, however, effective. There was never any doubt in the minds of Patton's audience, what he said and what he meant with his colorful language. In fact, he mentioned that "We can never get anything across unless we talk the language of the people we are trying to instruct. Perhaps that is why I curse."

To ensure that his order was understood, Patton always had the other person repeat the order back to him—another good idea for management to adopt:

> *If a unit must be withdrawn, see that all soldiers along the line of withdrawal are informed why it is taking place and when it will occur.*

Communicating plans to the employees, the company soldiers, especially when they are unexpected and negative in nature is essential to the efficient operation of the plan. (Unfortunately, an employee often discovers a company retrenchment program as he receives his lay-off notice.) Maybe Patton thought that word of mouth was the best method of getting things across, but American management has had little success in doing anything without a lot of paperwork. At times it seems American industry was built on paper, is maintained by paper, and cannot survive without it. Paperwork seems to react to a reverse utility curve. As the quantity of work decreases, the paperwork to control the work increases proportionally. And employees seem to have an almost natural predisposition toward the creation of paperwork.

For a long time, computer technology was advertised as the cure for unnecessary paperwork, but it seems to spawn new methods to create it. Where in the past there existed certain limitation on the storage of data that could be later transformed to paperwork, now we have, through advanced technology, the means to bypass the limitation with multigigabyte optical erasable disks. Now, anything can be stored regardless of worth and become the source of potential paperwork. Desk-top publishing, whereby using the miracles of computer technology just about anyone can become a publisher at a very low cost, is another source of increasing paperwork. Of course there are many benefits to these advances in storage and retrieval systems, nevertheless, the potential for unnecessary paperwork has skyrocketed.

THE MEMO

Much of the heralded unnecessary paperwork in business is in the form of memos to other people within earshot. The overt purpose is to initiate action, but two covert and more important purposes, in many instances, are to document and record some instance of the writer's managerial success and the failure on the part of some other manager. The distribution lists on memos of this nature are usually quite extensive and are directed toward the next higher level of management. The memo is also an excellent tool to document excuses of failure. The memo pulled from the files proves the allegation that the manager tried but other people failed to carry out his plan. Thus, he does not share responsibility for failure. Also, management expends money to provide employees with telephones, but their use in lieu of the office memo is skimpy. It appears that oral instruction can only be effective when issued by a confident manager.

Some managers use the memo in the same manner as the performer uses an agent. The agent spends his time keeping the performer's name and deeds in the public eye. The memo is the tool used by some to keep higher management apprised of the manager's name and deeds. Managers have resisted all attempts to limit, eliminate, or improve the use of the memo, and it seems that until its excessive use is recognized as a mark of the ineffective manager, its longevity is guaranteed. Efforts should be made, however, to reduce memo length so that it expresses intent with a minimum of verbiage. Patton wrote:

> There is nothing harsh in brief words of command any more than there is impoliteness in the brief wording of a telegram. Commands simply express your desire, your signal, in the briefest and most emphatic language possible. If you are to obtain obedience from your men, your language must express your meaning concisely and with emphasis and further, each meaning must always be expressed in precisely the same language.

Patton's memos and orders were always clearly understood and never wordy.

POLICIES AND PROCEDURES

Some form and quantity of company policy and procedure must exist even though their existence often draws criticism. Yet, the same people who criticize the very existence of written procedures would not tell the pilot of the airplane on which they are passengers to scrap his written preflight procedure. Procedures have their place. Consider the pandemonium that would exist if the Internal Revenue Service directed each citizen to submit an income tax return on April 15 of each year yet provided no guidelines, procedures, and forms for their submission. Procedures provide a guide for handling recurring tasks in an efficient manner that can reduce costly errors. Detractors argue that procedures inhibit creativity, restrict technical advances, and foster organizational robots. To a degree, this may be true, but the value of some organizational conformance and some creative inhibition may be far greater to the businessman than its absence is to the artist, psychologist, and sociologist.

But there is a danger where excessive policy and procedure manuals are produced and distributed. Printed procedures have an almost mystical quality of tradition and validity. Simply because something is in a procedures manual, the reader assumes it's correct, often at the expense of original thinking. If the detail is too great, all creativity ceases and mediocrity abounds.

Another danger is the temporary procedure written to provide guidance for temporary occurrences. Often the need for the procedures will pass quickly, but the procedure will last. There is nothing in business more permanent than a temporary procedure.

Patton had his procedures, instructions, and orders, but they were not issued in excess nor ever meant to convey the concept that independent thinkers were unwelcomed.

RECORDS RETENTION

Another source of wasteful paperwork are the pack-rat tendencies of most business managers to file every piece of written material that they have ever created or received. The origin of this strange phenomenon is unknown, but any manager will attest to that strange feeling of guilt when he tries to discard some form of written material for which he does not have a superseding copy. It's almost as though "collecting paper" is an unwritten but important objective of all organizations, and the quantity in file cabinets is a measure of job importance and magnitude. Some companies request that all file cabinets be purged of unnecessary paper annually. If only some method could be devised to prevent the paperwork from being filed in the first place. The files are purged, but rather than destroyed, the paperwork is filed in small packing boxes, specifically designed to save it forever, and carted off to a place called "the archives" which is usually a warehouse-type building, the location of which is known only to the records retention department. All of this costs money and represents waste.

The military doesn't seem to have a similar problem in that a combat vehicle such as a tank cannot accommodate too many file cabinets. The army does have records, but the mobility requirements of operational units restricts the quantity of paper retention. Perhaps, if managers had to load their filed papers into their cars on a monthly basis and store them at home the habit of collecting paper might subside.

The reason that paperwork excesses are so important is because of the large potential for waste. Early attention to cost-reduction programs were in the form of industrial and manufacturing engineering efforts, and for years improvements have been made in hardware design and production methods so that now little room exists for large-scale savings. Hardware is pretty efficient, but over the years, little has been done to reduce excessive paperwork costs. They have grown, untethered, to become a significant element of cost.

MEETINGS

Patton suggested that each echelon staff meet briefly *each day* to review operations. Although the exigencies of business are not comparable to those of war, a weekly staff meeting is seldom excessive in modern management. In many companies a daily staff meeting if kept to a reasonable and productive time period may not only be informative but also could aid in fostering better rapport among the staff. It may instill a team feeling and attitude. On the other hand, too many meetings can be detrimental. Sometimes executives convene meetings simply to satisfy their ego and show their power. Often these meetings are called at the dinner hour or some equally inconvenient time that would heighten the unproductiveness of the assembly. Meetings of this nature confuse whatever little planning exists and destroys morale.

Meetings are an excellent form of communicating ideas, policies, and directives, but unless the benefits exceed the cost they are questionable. Patton's staff meetings were always brief and to the point.

EMPLOYEE SUGGESTIONS

An employee suggestion program may seem, on the surface, to be an excellent source of improved communication between the employees and the company. It can be, if well thought out, well promulgated, and well managed, but the problems it can produce are overwhelming. If the program disperses money for the ideas based on the savings the idea generates, then the perils increase. The subjective nature of estimating the true source of the idea, and estimating a factual saving, can result in many dubious awards and occupy the time of many arguing managers.

The effect that a suggestion program can have on morale can be negative if the suggestions are not dealt with judiciously. The fact that on a national average about 75 percent of the suggestions received from employees are neither approved nor implemented is cause for concern. Seventy-five percent of the time the company is telling the employees that their ideas that they spent time developing are not valuable. If someone has discovered a method to reject an employee's idea and increase the employee's morale at the same time, this danger is averted. Until that time, extreme care should be exercised in establishing the ground rules and procedures for an employee suggestion system.

COMPANY ATTITUDE

As in the case of individuals, each company establishes and communicates to its employees a certain attitude. It can be a winning attitude, a losing attitude, or an in-between attitude. The corporate attitude can influence the attitude of the employees to either promote or retard business success. Each company has its own special personality that affects employees, customers, and competitors.

Patton said, "Wars are not won by defensive tactics," and he abhorred a defensive mentality. It showed in his tactics. Corporate management could learn from the General.

Many companies select a defensive position unknowingly by a combination of actions and policies. Patton violated the time-honored, much publicized, and almost instinctive drive to "dig in." He regarded a defensive position as a deterrent to goal attainment. He reasoned that (1) preparing a defensive position gave the enemy valuable time to better coordinate its advance and (2) the soldier was psychologically handicapped by digging in because he'd assume the enemy was present in overwhelming force.

In business, the defensive attitude is often evidenced by one or more of the following phrases.

"We tried that before."

"Our business is different."

"It costs too much."

"We're too busy to do that."

"It isn't in the budget."

"It's against company policy."

"It will run up our overhead."

"Why change? It's working OK."

"Let's get back to reality."

"That's not our problem."

"We've never done it before."

"We're too small for it."

"Upper management will never approve it."

Many contend that the tendency to resist change is a natural reaction. People don't like change. But an analysis of this resistance reveals that this is not always true. At least half the people listed in the divorce columns of newspapers desire change, and certainly new car buyers demonstrate a desire for change. The average Californian trades houses every four or five years. So there seem to be conditions under which change is not only acceptable, but desired. The conditions appear to be when someone has something to gain and nothing to lose from the change, and when the change is initiated by that someone. If the company can establish a positive attitude incorporating those conditions in the company philosophy, the employees will be able to identify potential roadblocks to plans and progress and in so doing avert roadblocks on the way to individual and company success.

The company that assumes or resigns itself to a static state, and does nothing to combat the natural apathy that sets in, cannot operate to optimum effectiveness. Employees with this defensive attitude will impede any planned progress by devising and building an almost impassable series of roadblocks. Meanwhile, the competition moves ahead.

Company attitude as an important contributor to employee-company communications and as a forceful marketing tool should not be taken lightly. It should appear as an agenda item for meetings of the board of directors.

SUMMARY

Companies have long given lip service to the importance of good communication with employees and with the public. Often, however, the *lack of communications* has served as the convenient excuse for major and minor mistakes at the lower management levels. The beauty of this excuse is that it did not pinpoint blame or accountability, and provided its own solution: "Improve avenues of communication."

Patton thought communication was a method of getting one person's ideas over to another person clearly, understandably. The suggestions he offered on how to accomplish this might easily be applied to a business setting. "Keeping the troops informed" in business is crucial to successful operations, and communicating company goals and objectives in a positive way is also required. To make sure that the recipient understood Patton's orders, he had the person repeat the order back to him. Managers could use that practice to advantage.

Company communications often involve excessive paperwork, which is unnecessary and adds to overhead. Company memos can be effective if kept short and to the point, but they can be misused by self-serving or vindictive managers. Policies and procedures can institutionalize the way things are done at the expense of original thinking. They can also be a source of unnecessary costs.

Employee suggestion programs can have a positive effect on the employee-company relations, but the potential perils to morale require serious caveats.

Meetings that are well-timed and attended by those that need to be present can be the most efficient means of communications, but like the memo they can be misused for personal reasons.

The attitude the company projects to the employees and to the public is an important asset to successful operations and deserves far more attention than it has received in the past. The company must establish the attitude of a winner.

PATTON SAID:	A GOOD MANAGER:
☐ "Use letters of instructions and personal conferences."	☐ Coordinates efforts prior to new directives.
☐ "Keep the troops informed.	☐ Tells *all* employees of the objectives, plans, and subsequent revision.
☐ "Issue orders by word of mouth."	☐ Doesn't document everything in memo form.
☐ "Talk the language of the people you are trying to instruct.	☐ Restricts use of country club language when employees don't understand it.
☐ "Brief words are not harsh or impolite."	☐ Doesn't orate unnecessarily.
☐ "Wars are not won by defensive tactics."	☐ Establishes and fosters a winning attitude.

Chapter 12
CONTROL

Find Out Where the War Is Today

Devising a plan is only five percent of the responsibility of command. The remaining ninety-five percent is to ensure that the plan is carried out.

In essence, the plan is the most important management function, because without a plan the remaining functions are useless. But the plan in itself is seldom sufficient to attain a goal. Someone has got to push it, or pull it, and make sure it works. The pushing, pulling, and assuring is called control. For Patton, it was a large and important part of command.

In business, at times, there seems to be an excess of control functions. We have production control, inventory control, change control, material control, financial control, and a host of other so-called control functions. When a problem with control exists, it often is with "overcontrol." Management needs to determine if the control functions that exist ensure that the plan works or are only part of the control function—such as the reporting part. Is the amassing of after-the-fact data that explain why the plan didn't work the core of control? Or is the essence of control a more active than passive action?

It might satisfy curiosity to examine the financial statements after bankruptcy procedures have begun to determine why bankruptcy occurred, but it would have been far more beneficial if the statements had been timely enough to warn of impending bankruptcy. If an alarm, warning of conditions that would lead to bankruptcy, were given, then planning or replanning could have been initiated to avert the disaster.

Patton believed that the function of control was to ensure that the events that occurred conformed to the plan that he had devised, and although he was an ardent student of history, he seldom confused history with control. To him, control was something that told him something would happen before it happened, or, at its worst, that it was in fact happening. If it told him something happened after-the-fact, it was no longer control. Then it was history.

Patton's attitude toward the techniques of control raises many provocative questions concerning the usual and often pedantic approach used today in management to fulfill the concept of control. For instance, the quality-control function may measure the effectiveness of that particular department with charts depicting failure rates, scrap factors, rejection rates, and other negative aspects. If quality-control supervisors uncovered a multitude of marginal products, rejected a larger quantity of parts, stopped shipment of some finished goods, and in general irritated a few of the producers, they would consider their effectiveness high. Their identifiable output is reflected in the data on the charts and indicates a determined effort and action on the part of the quality control personnel. Their data then become the justification for the organization's existence. If detection of errors were the only function of the control process, then they have truly performed their jobs. But assuring that the product-quality aspects of the company's plan were being accomplished is not enough. Quality-control personnel should also engage in preventive-quality action, internal-correction action, external-correction action, and assess the optimum cost effectiveness of each. The estimated industry's quality cost is 15 to 20 percent of the cost of sales—a significant cost contribution. It would be reasonable to consider that a larger investment in the preventive end of the quality cycle should reduce the magnitude of the correction action, thereby decreasing the total quality cost and increasing customer satisfaction. This would constitute the quality process of control.

INFORMATION

The control of a plan is based on constant measurement of the situation now compared to what the plan says the situation should now be.

The difference, if any, is the magnitude of the problem. The measurement task is normally based on information received from many sources, and Patton had a lot to say about reporting and interpreting information as well as the application of good judgment:

> *Good judgment comes from experience and experience comes from poor judgment.*

Patton was not an advocate of tomes of position papers. He liked brief reports and thought that reports or orders that required more than one side of one page indicated confused and indecisive thinking. His favorite story used to illustrate this point was a report from a sentinel who intercepted German paratroopers in the Bastogne area wearing U.S. uniforms. The report read: "One sentinel, reinforced, stopped seventeen Germans in U.S. uniforms. Fifteen were shot and two died suddenly."

In business, this cryptic message might be expanded somewhat, and a management report of the situation would probably read quite differently:

> *Considerable progress has been made in the preliminary work directed toward the establishment of criteria to identify, classify, and otherwise define undocumented military personnel who have assumed the outward appearance of company personnel.*
>
> *Considerable difficulty has been encountered in the selection of statistically valid criteria but experimental methods are being employed to optimize this effort. In this report period, one incursion of aforementioned undocumented personnel was encountered by a member of the task team established by the steering committee. The results of the confrontation are being analyzed by the systems analysis group and preliminary indications are favorable. It now appears that between fifteen and twenty incursion personnel were treated in this incident and their efficacy to offset company objectives has been neutralized. A complete analysis will be presented within six months from the date of this report.*
>
> *It is expected that the rate of progress shall continue to accelerate as policy definition is attained and additional*

> *knowledgeable personnel are budgeted for the systems
> analysis group.*

The translation may seem excessive even for comparison purposes, but writing with this "fog content" does exist in abundance. The old saying "Write to express not to impress" may be fine for business school courses in effective writing, but the "real world" of management contains many frustrated Hemingways who spend their working lives composing writing that is less intelligible than the example.

REPORTS

Patton was well aware that the validity of reported data had to be assessed:

> *In war nothing is ever as bad, or as good as it is reported
> to Higher Headquarters. Any report which emanates after
> dark . . . should be viewed with skepticism by the next
> higher unit. Reports by wounded men are always exagger-
> ated and favor the enemy.*

He restricted his remarks to war, only because he had never occupied a corporate position. With minor rewording, his advice is quite applicable to business: substituting *business* for *war, higher management* for *higher headquarters, in the dark* for *after dark, failures* for *wounded men,* and *competition* for *enemy*:

> *In business nothing is ever as bad or as good as it is re-
> ported to higher management. Any report which emanates
> in the dark . . . should be viewed with skepticism by upper
> management. Reports by those who have failed in their task
> are always exaggerated in favor of competitors.*

For some reason, a report that is printed, or better yet, one that is computer generated, is always believed. Computers never lie. If the report is bound and includes a generous sprinkling of charts and graphs, even the most skeptical is silenced. This almost mystical quality of the printed word, contrasted to the spoken word that is always taken with a grain of salt, often constitutes blind faith. This blind faith has been the cause of many erroneous and costly decisions.

The conditions under which the basic reported data have been collected and compiled deserves at least a cursory examination for possible bias. Data, after all, are evaluated subjectively. Even the pure science of mathematics is suspect especially when statistics are used to justify a position. Unfortunately, most managers have forgotten the ingredients of a valid statistical analysis. To support their arguments, they simply collect and exercise those data that prove their point. Advertising firms are masters of this art: "Two out of every three doctors contacted picked dingles over the competitive product." (In reality, only three doctors were contacted and they held mail-order degrees in divinity from Shoeless Joe Jackson University in California.)

Statistics, graphs, and charts are beneficial tools when used correctly, but through habit many managers unquestioningly accept these graphic metaphors as evidence of excellent planning and thorough job knowledge. Each instance should be examined.

Reports from managers who have failed to complete an assigned task often overstate the complexities of the task and the problems encountered. It's human nature. Man will not fashion the club with which he is about to be beaten. Also, Patton mentioned that tired division commanders are always pessimists and perhaps similar conditions exist in the reports of tired executives.

DISCRIMINATION

Patton once made a very interesting observation on discrimination:

> *When you receive reports of counter-attacks find out who sent them—that is, the size of the unit which sent them. A squad occupying a position will report an enemy section approaching it as a counter-attack, But such a counter-attack has no material effect on a division or a corps.*

One of the most important qualities of a good manager is the ability to discern between the important and the unimportant matters so that time and resources can be allocated accordingly. The effect that a reported incident has on the total organization should be considered in perspective to avoid inordinate expense of time and cost. It is not uncommon in the annals of business to uncover an instance or two where a manager or a vice president is confronted with a reported rare omission that may have cost the company $1,000. Since it is rare, it is more irritating than costly. The manager or vice president will react with a thunderous order to his subordinates, "Don't let me ever see this happen again." In response the subordinate will really make sure that the boss never sees that again. They'll establish plans, control systems, computer reports, and even whole departments to assure that it never, never happens again. The net effect is that a $100,000 control system will be established to avert a $1,000 error that might occur once a year. These needless control systems are not isolated instances and one does not have to look very far to spot several in any business. If these systems are reduced to automation and issued on at least six-part computer paper, synergistic effects can be observed. From meaningless data, an entire department can be built. It seems that very little resistance to automating any data is ever encountered. Some automated control systems have the survivability of the flatworm. They can be cut into many pieces, but instead of expiring, each piece survives as the basis of a new control system.

As in planning, the magnitude of the control function must be in proportion to the planned event. Excessive controls, a common business error, can be wasteful and inadequate controls, even more so. Selecting the right measure—which will most likely vary with each plan—is a judgment call and requires more of the art of management rather than the science of management.

INTELLIGENCE

In order to measure progress toward the plan, data must be gathered that validity portrays circumstances as they exist now. From that, data projections of what will exist tomorrow are developed. There are many sources of company internal data but when measuring market performance, which is an essential business plan, companies usually assign this intelligence-gathering function to their market-research function. The market research department amasses industry data from many and diverse sources, analyzes the data, and prepares situation reports for higher management. However, since the reporting of market research department may not be given the credence of expert information from outside the company, much of the offered intelligence may be discounted in favor of industry reports published by alleged authorities in the field.

The electronics industry offers an excellent example. There are a dozen or so companies whose main product consists of reports (in depth, of course) on specific computer products with charts and graphs, comparisons and analyses. These are issued annually, cost a lot of money, and become the industry standard. On the basis of these reports, companies assess their positions, products, goals, and objectives and revise their plans accordingly. Few question the validity of the data. After all, it is in print and even bound.

Some of these authorities gather their data by sending a questionnaire to all of the manufacturers of a specific item of computer-related hardware such as a digitizer. The questionnaire requests performance data, units in the field, new products introduced or about to be introduced, equipment price, and other data that might interest a prospective buyer. Since many of the manufacturers do not want to give the competitors accurate comparison data, the president of a small private company might direct that the questionnaire be answered with somewhat erroneous data. The question "How many operating units in the field?" might be answered "250," even though there are none presently in the field. The logic used in giving this answer would be: "The report won't be published for a year and by that time we plan to have 125 units in the field, so let's double that to scare our competitors." The other questions are answered with the same degree of honesty.

The publisher tabulates the results of the questionnaire, prepares an analysis concerning the tremendous growth factor of the market, and publishes the volume one year after the data is collected.

Now the president of the same small company that promoted the inaccuracies in his questionnaire reads the published report but forgets that the competitors are not dim witted and that they too may bend the truth for the same reasons. Yet, he may favor the published data over his own market research group, which has more reliable and current data input.

When Patton selected a staff intelligence officer, he believed the intelligence reports. He selected this officer very carefully and considered his selections to be the best in the business. One morning after an air raid, Patton's intelligence officer, Colonel Oscar Koch, summarized the raid. "The antiaircraft people say that forty-five German bombers came over last night and that they shot down fifteen. Allowing for the slight percentage error occasionally present in such reports, we conclude that fifteen planes came over and that they shot down three."

That's exactly what a good intelligence group can do—filter and factor incoming data until they represent actual conditions. Patton was always disputing any data received or used by the Soviets especially in regard to the masses of German troops encircling Stalingrad. He claimed that there

were a lot more Russians than there were Germans. He believed that the
Russians were feeding a lot of propaganda and that the Americans were
believing it. He told his nephew:

> *Well, take the German troops occupying France, Norway,*
> *Belgium, and other places, then take the ones fighting in*
> *Africa, the ones in reserve training center in Germany, and*
> *the ones that must be elsewhere on the Russian front, add*
> *them all up and subtract the total from the maximum num-*
> *ber of military age males in a country of 75 million. Even*
> *assuming that not a single man of fighting age is a factory*
> *worker, you'll see what I mean. There just cannot possibly*
> *be the number of Nazi troops in Russia that our Red friends*
> *claim; and there can't be that many facing Montgomery*
> *either. We're doing it again. We're taking counsel of our*
> *fears and scaring hell out of ourselves.*

The same analysis could have been made on the aforementioned digitizer example. If these estimates were to be believed, each household in
America would have to be housing a digitizer.

In his *Real-World Intelligence* (Weidenfeld & Nicholson, 1988), Her-
bert E. Meyer, a former CIA manager, explains the importance of intelligence operations—not spying—as a management tool. He warns that
unless business executives actively design intelligence-gathering departments, their survival could be jeopardized. He reveals how and why Japanese companies such as Mitsubishi have been collecting public-source
intelligence for years and that Mitsubishi Corporation intelligence staff
occupies two floors of a Manhattan skyscraper.

A maxim of military intelligence states: "To estimate what the enemy
hopes or intends to do next, look to see what he is making the maximum
effort to find out." This could very well be extended to today's domestic
and international business. An intelligence officer in business is going to
be a necessity. As Patton said, "I ought to know what I'm doing. I have
the best damned intelligence officer in any U.S. command."

SECURITY

Data security has become a very serious problem for companies and
especially serious for those whose data are stored in computer memory.
Shredding machine stock constitutes a good investment now that many

highly paid executives are engaged in cutting up unimportant memos, financial sheets, and miscellaneous scratch-pad paper into tiny shreds. This may be a ridiculous degree of security, but sometimes security is required because people are stealing data.

Complex security systems are being developed to prevent or at least impede such data piracy, but the cost of these systems in terms of extra memory, increased computer overhead, decreased acquisition time and development time is staggering. As soon as a software security system is developed and offered for sale, some computer hacker develops a system to offset it. Some companies just haven't considered security yet because the horse has yet to be stolen.

Rather than spending money to provide protection for all stored data, a selective process could be used. Then only the data that could be used to advantage by the competitors need be protected. This concept might appear so evident that it shouldn't even be discussed, yet many companies are spending money to protect data that needs no protection.

Patton practiced security precautions in a selective way, especially in communications. Rather than coding each message automatically, he applied a very simple rule:

> *If the period of action is shorter than the period of reaction, use clear; otherwise use code. By this I mean that if you tell a combat team to attack at 1000 hours and your experience shows that the enemy cannot react to the information until 1100, use clear.*

An example of this would be product data relating to a product with a planned marketing life of two years. If it would take competitors a minimum of three years to tool-up, produce, and market the product even with the design data, the cost of protecting the data would be wasteful. If the response time was half that, then some measure of security may be prudent. Data should be examined in view of their potential use to others and the cost of protection. If the consequence of failure to protect it is lower than the cost to protect it, forget it.

SEEING IS BELIEVING

Patton was always trying "to find out where the war is today." It wasn't that he distrusted his intelligence, it was just that seeing for himself somehow gave him a better perspective on the total action. Charts, graphs, and reports are invaluable in the control function, but sometimes one look is worth a thousand pictures. You get the feel of the situation in all its aspects. Business managers should also "find out where the war is today" by getting around to as many remote company offices as reasonably possible and speaking with the employees engaged in front-line selling or other front-line activity. Besides the morale factors involved, a manager can learn many revealing things in speaking to the troops.

In July 1944, Patton visited the headquarters of an armored division halted on the road. He observed the division commander and his staff enmeshed in a map study of the possibility of crossing the Seine River. Patton glanced at the map, and walked down to the river. He found it two feet deep and defended by a single machine gun, which, he said, ". . . missed me by a good deal." He went back and asked the division commanding general why he didn't get across the river. The division commander replied that he didn't know whether the tide was in or out and that he understood that the river was strongly defended. Patton wrote, "I told him in very strong language what I had just done and to get a move on himself, which he did." Patton believed in going out and looking around.

WALKING IN THE OTHER GUY'S SHOES

One of Patton's precepts of command was, "Put yourself in the shoes of your subordinate," and he practiced it in Georgia, California, North Africa, Sicily, France, and Germany. At unannounced times he would take over the functions of the duty officer or the officer of the day at his headquarters. He said, "I don't really do it to scare anybody but I must admit, I managed to keep some of my juniors on their goddamned toes."

There isn't much business precedence for "stepping into the subordinate's shoes" but it could offer a revealing perspective from the "other guys" point of view. In addition, it might gratify the subordinate when his manager announces, "Go play golf for the day, I'll take over here." It's difficult to imagine the impact on company management when the word gets around. It couldn't be all bad. Most likely, the subordinate would be motivated to have his organization always prepared for such an eventuality and therefore always performing efficiently.

At St. Joseph's Hospital and Medical Center in Phoenix, Arizona, Dr. Charles Daschbach initiated a program as part of the medical education system called "White Shoes." As part of the program, staff physicians and

interns followed nurses on their rounds to increase the doctors understanding of the nurses responsibilities. The program appears to be successful. Dr. Daschbach renewed his skills by checking patient's vital signs
and learned to chart them on volumes of paper. He also observed the
stoic nerves of a good nurse. "I was kind of scared. I was way over my
head," Dr. Daschbach said. That program, renamed "Walk in My Shoes
Day" was expanded to thirty-eight other Arizona hospitals. George Patton would have approved.

KEEPING SCORE

Patton was almost fanatical in monitoring his progress by keeping
score:

> *In order to know constantly the situation, two sets of ca-
> sualty reports, both enemy and our own, must be kept.*

To Patton, counting dead and wounded was not a macabre pastime,
but something ingrained in American youth since the invention of baseball. Patton was keeping score of the game—hits, runs, and errors. From
this score he constantly appraised his game plan. He kept score of the
dead, wounded, prisoners taken, and vehicles destroyed, and compared
these data with his own losses. He would then subtract the enemy losses
from what he believed their total pool of resources and then figured that
he had a pretty good appraisal of how the war was going.

He was very careful with these data and very persistent. The raw data
were presented daily during combat and factored by his intelligence officer. They appeared as:

THIRD ARMY		ENEMY	
Killed	21,098	Killed	138,700
Wounded	97,163	Wounded	369,700
Missing	16,393	Prisoners	545,800
Total	134,654	Total	1,054,200
Nonbattle	106,440		
Casualties			
GRAND TOTAL	241,094		

MATERIAL LOSSES

Light tanks	298	Medium tanks	1,492
Medium tanks	934	Panther or tiger tanks	857
Guns	174	Guns	3,324

Patton kept a running total and constantly reappraised his positions. Football teams maintain similar data from which the coaches, owners, sportswriters, and fans can assess the teams effectively:

		US		THEM
Ground gained rushing		130		100
Ground gained passing		275		190
Total ground gained		405		290
Penalties	(5)	50	(4)	45
Turnovers		2		3
Score		28		14

In business, sometimes we forget to keep score and wait until the end of the game to find out whether we won or lost. For example, a business may have an objective to capture 50 percent of a specific market. (More often, the objective is less definitive—as "increase our market share by year end.") In order to determine the score at any time, the manager must know the sales of each competitor to that point, calculate his present share, compare it to previous shares, and ensure progress to his objective. If he finds that he is losing ground, then he must replan to offset the difference and revise his objective. He can't afford to wait for year-end reports. Yet since waiting for year-end reporting seems to be the easiest method of appraisal, it usually predominates—in those instances, that is, where it is done at all. Business seems to have a great deal of work to do to approach Patton's concepts and practices of control.

Patton knew his position in comparison to where he planned to be and in comparison to where the enemy was positioned at all times. From his scorecard, he could also forecast the most probable positions in the near future.

SUMMARY

The techniques of modern management control, especially when computers are involved, often fail to achieve their purpose. Where data collection, sorting, and analysis have been simplified and cost has been reduced, it often seems that the control function depends upon how much data can be creatively interpreted and how many easy answers can be printed out. This approach detracts from the concept, "Where am I in relation to where I'm going?"

The essence of control is monitoring progress, evaluating the source of data input, and in interpreting the input in relation to what actually exists. Patton understood this and knew how to train his subordinates to evaluate information effectively. That's why he never lost a battle.

MAKING SURE IT WORKS

PATTON SAID:	A GOOD MANAGER:
☐ "Making sure it works is 95% of command responsibility."	☐ Treats the control function as a dynamic rather than static function.
☐ "Nothing is ever as good or as bad as it is reported."	☐ Uses experience and judgment to evaluate reports.
☐ "Find out the size of the unit that sent the report."	☐ Defines and considers the source of the report.
☐ "Trust your intelligence staff."	☐ Doesn't discount company research efforts in favor of suspect industry reports.
☐ "If the period of reaction is longer than the period of action, do not use code."	☐ Doesn't use data security measures on things that cannot help competition in a timely manner.
☐ "Put yourself in the other guy's shoes."	☐ Takes over a subordinate's job occasionally.

PATTON SAID:	A GOOD MANAGER:
☐ "Keep score."	☐ Compares progress continually to the best available data on the competition.
☐ "Don't direct units from a map."	☐ Goes to see what's going on.

EPILOGUE

Certainly General Patton did not have all the answers to all of management's problems, but those that he did face have so many parallels in management today that his views fairly demand consideration. His practical suggestions and approaches are so sound that the manager who emulates him would undoubtedly profit.

Management is not a true science and Patton made the observation, "War is an art and as such is not susceptible to explanation by fixed formulae." If Patton was correct about his many previous lives, then maybe, just maybe, somewhere in American management circles is a tall, thin, 44-year-old successful executive, walking through his factory with a military gait, saying, "Management is an art and as such is not susceptible to explanation by fixed formulae."

INDEX